Book 3

STEEL
ON
STEEL

Bill Perkins

Compass Publishing
a division of
Compass International, Inc.
Coeur d'Alene, Idaho
compass.org

STEEL ON STEEL

Book 3

Compass Publishing, Inc.
Coeur d'Alene, Idaho
www.compass.org
© Copyright 2020 All rights reserved.
First Printing September 2020
Printed in the United States of America.

ISBN-10: 1-57437-193-2
ISBN-13: 978-1-57437-193-2

Cover and interior design by Gordon McDonald, GoGo Design.

All proceeds from the purchase of this book go to Compass Publishing,
a division of Compass Int'l, Inc., Coeur d'Alene, Idaho, compass.org.

CONTENTS

CONTENTS

PREFACE

Put on the full armor of God, so that you will be able to stand firm against the schemes of the devil. Eph. 6:11

The world is quickly changing—Satan is no longer hiding in the closet or lurking in the shadows. Rather, he's quite in the open about his agenda...which is first and foremost to get our eyes off God and His principles.

Our only true defense in the days in which we live is knowing well the Word of God. When we know our Bible well, we can do all things through Him who strengthens us. Apart from Him, we are no match against the wiles of the devil.

So this book, Steel on Steel 3, delves deeply into Scriptural truths meant to armor you up for this unique day and time. There are over 500 verses noted to help motivate you to be used by Him.

May the Lord use you mightily as we wind up the Age of the Church and loudly exit this earth into His presence.

Shalom!

CHAPTER ONE

THE POOL OF SILOAM
AND THE MESSIAH

On our trips to Israel, my most enjoyable Bible study to teach is from the top of the Mount of Olives. The view of the Old City is stupendously visually impacting to anyone with even a basic understanding of the Bible.

You can literally see so many of the things mentioned in Scripture like the Garden of Gethsemane, Palm Sunday Road, the Eastern Gate, the Temple Mount where the Jewish Temple stood, Caiaphas' House, the Garden Tomb, the City of David, Herod's Palace, and so much more.

One of the more interesting observations I like to point out from this breathtaking view from the Mount of Olives is the famous story of Jesus healing a beggar who was blind from birth (John 8:59-9:41).

In a nutshell, Jesus was leaving the Temple compound, saw the blind beggar, picked up some dirt, spit into the dirt, and applied it to the beggar's eyes.

He told the beggar to go wash the dirt out of his eyes in the Pool of Siloam. And once he did, he could instantly see for the first time in his life.

The Pharisees came to the beggar to question him about Jesus healing him. They were unmercifully berating the poor guy about how this could have happened, ultimately resulting in the healed man blurting out the now-famous words, *"All I know is that I was blind but now I can see."*

Why did Jesus send the blind beggar all the way to the Pool of Siloam?

More to the story

But when you're sitting on the Mount of Olives reading this Biblical account, you learn there's a lot more to the story. You can see the place where the stunning Jewish Temple once stood (#1 in graphic, right). Jesus would have been in that area when He healed the blind beggar. Only a couple of hundred feet to the north, just outside the northern wall of the Temple Mount, were the Pools of Bethesda, a relatively short, flat walk (#2 in the graphic, right).

But Jesus didn't send the poor blind beggar to the Pools of Bethesda, only a short distance away. Instead He said, "Go wash in the Pool of Siloam," which was five times farther away down to the lowest part of Jerusalem (#3 in the graphic, right). For a blind guy, that was a LONG way to go— especially since the Pools of Bethesda were so much closer.

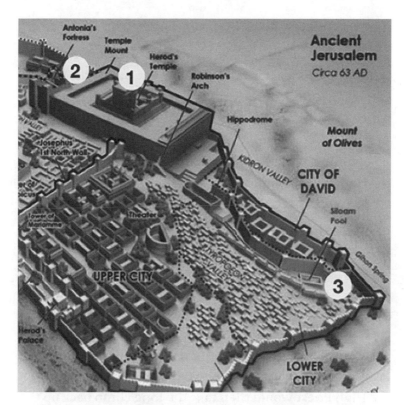

Why did Jesus send the blind beggar all the way to the Pool of Siloam? Well, as the Scripture points out, the Pool of Siloam's name in Hebrew means "The Pool of the One Who Will Be Sent," which was, of course, the Messiah. The Jews regarded this pool as prophetic of the Messiah pouring water upon the desert.

The Pool of Siloam was also symbolic of the Messiah pouring out the Holy Spirit on the Jews. The blind beggar was told to go to the Messiah's pool to be healed. The name of the specific location the blind beggar was told to go to in order to be healed would not have been missed by the Pharisees.

But there's even more to the story...

Each fall the Jews celebrate the Feast of Tabernacles. The last day of this feast is called "The Great Day of the Feast." On this day, the priests would perform a special ritual in which the nation would cry out for their Messiah to come.

Beginning at the Temple located at the top of Mt. Moriah, the High Priest would lead a long line of priests as they sang their way down a wide descending boulevard (see picture on previous page) to the Pool of Siloam, located at the bottom of Mt. Moriah.

The clean water flowing onto the blood-soaked altar...

At the pool the High Priest would fill a special pitcher with water. With great pomp and ceremony, leading a large group of priests, Pharisees, Sadducees, and Scribes, the High Priest would then take the long climb back up the boulevard to the Temple at the top of Mount Moriah.

Entering the Gate Beautiful, through the Women's Court and into the male-only area of sacrifice, the High Priest would then take the pitcher of water to the Brazen Altar of Sacrifice located in front of the Temple entrance. He would pour the Pool of Siloam water from the pitcher on the altar while reading Isaiah 44:3 about the future Messiah coming to Israel:

For I will pour out water on the thirsty land and streams on the dry ground; I will pour out My Spirit on

your offspring and My blessing on your descendants...
Isa. 44:3

The clean water flowing onto the blood-soaked altar was an amazing visual that their sinless Messiah would come as the final and permanent sacrifice for sin.

The crowd would fall silent as they prayed for the Messiah to come and pour His Spirit on them. But this particular year, Jesus had come stealthily to Jerusalem without His Apostles (John 7:10).

And it was at this moment He boldly broke the prayerful silence by loudly proclaiming:

...If anyone is thirsty, let him come to Me and drink. He who believes in Me, as the Scripture said, "From his innermost being will flow rivers of living water."
Jn. 7:37-38

...was an amazing visual that their sinless Messiah would come as the final and permanent sacrifice for sin.

Jesus was answering their cry for their Messiah to come! The prophetic ritual of pouring the water from the Pool of the One Who Is Sent onto the altar and praying for their Messiah to redeem them had been answered!

But the crowd was confused. Some were amazed by His miracles and teaching. Others were adamant He was not the Messiah because He was from, they thought, Galilee and the Messiah was prophesied to be born in Bethlehem. They didn't realize He was actually born in Bethlehem.

The next day Jesus showed up at the Temple and confounded the Pharisees with His incredible oratory. Not being able to answer, they made a deep, deep dig at Jesus being born of fornication—supposing Mary had gotten pregnant by someone other than Joseph (or by Joseph before their wedding). Then they said He had a demon. Finally they tried to stone Him.

He tells him to go wash in the Pool of Siloam—The Pool of the Sent One.

Jesus slipped away from their grasp, and as He left the Temple area, he saw the blind beggar sitting on the sidewalk. I have to think Jesus was smiling as He healed him right under their Pharisaical noses ...and then tells him to go wash in the Pool of Siloam—The Pool of the Sent One.

Now you know why Jesus didn't send the blind beggar to the close-by Pools of Bethesda!

CHAPTER TWO

BIBLICAL DISPENSATIONS

I f you're not a dispensationalist, you've got big problems regarding how you understand your Bible! Biblical dispensations are divinely ordained and easily distinguishable time periods prevailing throughout the Bible. And understanding them clears up so many so-called "problem verses."

In a nutshell, a dispensationalist believes God doesn't change but that He does change how He deals with people on the earth. So when you read your Bible, to understand the context you need to understand to whom each verse is directed—and in which time period or dispensation.

For instance, in Matthew, a book describing Jesus in-teracting with the Jews before the cross, Jesus says your forgiveness depends on what you do ... if you forgive, then you'll be forgiven.

> *For if you forgive others for their transgressions, your heavenly Father will also forgive you. But if you do not forgive others, then your Father will not forgive your transgressions. Matt. 6:14-15*

Yet 30 years later, in Paul's post-cross letter to the Ephesians, he says you've already been forgiven—clearly written in past tense.

> *Be kind to one another, tender-hearted, forgiving each other, just as God in Christ also has forgiven you. Eph. 4:32*

God didn't contradict Himself. He just dealt differently with people living before the cross than those living after the cross. We see seven of these distinguishing time periods/dispensations in the Bible. (See color bookmark inside cover.)

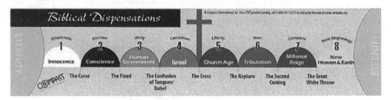

Looking at the above dispensation chart , you can see these seven dispensations. God dealt differently with Adam before and after he sinned. God dealt differently with people on earth before and after the global flood as well as before and after the Tower of Babel.

And as we just saw regarding forgiveness, God deals differently with people before and after the cross. He will deal differently with people before and after the Rapture and before and after the Second Coming. This is fact, not theory.

> *God deals differently with people before and after the cross.*

Notice it's the cross that is the dividing line between Israel and the Church Age, not Matthew 1. This is because Matthew, Mark, Luke, and John are accounts of Jesus interacting with people living under the Jewish Law, prior to the cross. So the main Bible divider should be Acts 2, not Matthew 1.

Here's an example of why it's critical to read your Bible via dispensations when interpreting Bible prophecy. Many non-dispensational teachers have taught that one of the prerequisites to the return of the Lord is that the Gospel must first be preached to every nation on earth—based on this verse:

> *This gospel of the kingdom shall be preached in the whole world as a testimony to all the nations, and then the end will come. Matt. 24:14*

There are some large national ministries that use this verse to fundraise for world evangelism, interpreting it to mean Jesus can't come until the entire world has heard the gospel. But trust me, there's no way God is sitting around waiting for sinful humans to evangelize every nation before He can act.

The fact is, this verse is written to the Jews under the Law regarding the future Tribulation dispensation which they will endure. It is not written to us living in the Church Age. And during the Tribulation, every nation in the world WILL hear the gospel preached by an angel from the sky:

And I saw another angel flying in midheaven, having an eternal gospel to preach to those who live on the earth, and to every nation and tribe and tongue and people... Rev. 14:6

But with Jesus' shed blood, a completely new dispensation began.

Dispensations clear up so many seeming contradictions in the Bible. When Jesus was on the earth, He was teaching and interacting with the Jews who were under the Law.

But with Jesus' shed blood, a completely new dispensation began. It was the mystery hidden in the Old Testament.

...the mystery which has been hidden from the past ages and generations... Col. 1:26

God appointed Paul to teach us this new understanding and application. But even Peter had a hard time understanding the dispensational change!

...as also in all his [Paul's] letters, speaking in them of

*these things, in which are some things **hard to understand...** 2Pet. 3:16*

Consider these examples of how things changed from before the cross to after the cross:

Israel Dispensation

...the way you judge, you will be judged... Matt. 7:2

Church Age Dispensation

...let us not judge one another anymore... Rom. 14:13

Israel Dispensation

...it is the one who has endured to the end who will be saved. Matt. 10:22

Church Age Dispensation

...you have been saved through faith...not as a result of works... Eph. 2:8,9

Israel Dispensation

...where two or three have gathered...I am there in their midst. Matt. 18:20

Church Age Dispensation

...do you not recognize this about yourselves, that Jesus Christ is in you...? 2Cor. 13:5

Israel Dispensation

...if you do not forgive others, then your Father will not forgive your transgressions. Matt. 6:15

Church Age Dispensation

Be kind to one another, tender-hearted, forgiving each other, just as God in Christ also has forgiven you. Eph. 4:32

Israel Dispensation

...everyone who divorces his wife, except for the reason of unchastity, makes her commit adultery... Matt. 5:32

Church Age Dispensation

Husbands, love your wives, just as Christ also loved the church... Eph. 5:25

The word mystery in the Greek is *mysterion,* and it means "truth undiscoverable except by divine revelation."

We have the divine Holy Spirit living in us so we can now understand deep truths that people in the Old Testament simply could not understand.

...the mystery which for ages has been hidden... Eph. 3:9

Once you have a comfortable grasp of dispensational theology, you'll have a solid Biblical foundation to build on to grow solidly in God's Word!

CHAPTER THREE

NOAH'S FLOOD:
FACT OR FICTION?

Noah's flood really did happen. To deny it's a real event, accurately recorded in Scripture, is to deny the trustworthiness of the entire Bible.

Noah's Flood is NOT a fable, myth or parable, and Christians need to know how to answer the most basic questions that people raise regarding this incredible event.

Let's begin with a quick summary of the events.

*God said to Noah, "The end of all flesh has come before Me; for **the earth is filled with violence** because of them; and behold, I am about to destroy them with the earth." Gen. 6:13*

*Behold, I, even **I am bringing the flood of water upon the earth, to destroy all flesh** in which is the breath of life, from under heaven; everything that is on the earth shall perish. Gen. 6:17*

Make for yourself an ark of gopher wood; you shall make the ark with rooms, and shall cover it inside and out with pitch. Gen. 6:14

*Then the LORD said to Noah, **"Enter the ark, you and all your household, for you alone I have seen to be righteous** before Me in this time. You shall take with you of every clean **animal** by sevens, a male and his female; and of the animals that are not clean two, a male and his female; also of the **birds** of the sky, by sevens, **male and female, to keep offspring alive** on the face of all the earth." Gen. 7:1-3*

> ### *... the fountains of the great deep burst open, and the floodgates of the sky were opened.*

*... the **fountains of the great deep burst open, and the floodgates of the sky were opened.** The rain fell upon the earth for forty days and forty nights. Gen. 7:11-12*

*The water prevailed more and more upon the earth, so that **all the high mountains everywhere under the heavens were covered.** Gen 7:19*

*God remembered Noah and all the beasts and all the cattle that were with him in the ark; and God caused a wind to pass over the earth, and **the water subsided.** Gen. 8:1*

*In the seventh month, on the seventeenth day of the
month, **the ark rested** upon the mountains of Ararat.
Gen. 8:4*

*Then God spoke to Noah, saying, **"Go out of the ark,**
you and your wife and your sons and your sons' wives
with you. Bring out with you every living thing of all
flesh that is with you, birds and animals and every
creeping thing that creeps on the earth, that they may
breed abundantly on the earth, and be fruitful and
multiply on the earth." Gen. 8:15-17*

If you believe in Biblical inerrancy, the Scriptural account
of this worldwide flood is not hard to believe. Our Creator
God, Who spoke the universe into being, can do anything
He wishes. (Psalm 33:6-9)

From the scientific side,
we know the entire earth
could be flooded because
God originally created the
earth as a planet of all water.

> *Our Creator God, Who
> spoke the universe into
> being, can do anything
> He wishes.*

*The earth was formless and void, and darkness was
over the surface of the deep, and the Spirit of God was
moving over the surface of the waters. Gen 1:2*

On day two of the Creation week, the wording indicates
a lot of the earth's water was taken up into the clouds.
Some have theorized that this was a sort of vapor canopy

and it shielded the sun's rays... possibly the reason people lived longer in those days.

> *...the earth was formed **out of water** and by water...*
> *2Pet. 3:5*

> *Then God said, "Let there be an expanse in the midst of the waters, and let it **separate the waters from the waters.**" God made the expanse, and separated the waters which were below the expanse from the waters which were above the expanse; and it was so. God called the expanse heaven. And there was evening and there was morning, a second day. Gen. 1:6-8*

It's quite humorous that you hear the claim from scientists that Mars was at one time flooded with water.

There's not a drop of water on Mars today, and they think somehow it was once flooded!

But the earth, with 5/6 of the planet covered with water today, they claim couldn't have had a worldwide flood? Please, where is the common sense?

Realistically, all this is simply an attack on God and His authority. They don't want to admit that God can do anything He wants, anytime He wants. If they admit to there being a God, then they have to ask: What does He want, what are His rules, who goes to heaven, etc.

On the other hand, if you believe God's Word as fact, you trust God created the heavens and the earth by speaking them into existence.

> *...God, who...calls into being that which does not exist. Rom. 4:17*

We can never truly grasp that belief because we're mere mortals with limited brains and understanding. So it's not necessary that we totally understand everything about how or why God does what He does.

> **The secret things belong to the LORD** *our God, but the things revealed belong to us and to our sons forever, that we may observe all the words of this law. Deut. 29:29*

> *He has made everything appropriate in its time. He has also set eternity in their heart, yet so that **man will not find out the work which God has done** from the beginning even to the end. Eccl. 3:11*

But God says we can trust what He reveals in His Word to be true. So we do, believing and defending every Word of the Bible, including the account of the worldwide flood.

And we're in good company—Jesus Himself talked about a literal worldwide flood.

> *For the coming of the Son of Man will be just like the days of Noah. For as in those days before the flood they were eating and drinking, marrying and giving in marriage, until the day that Noah entered the ark, and they did not understand **until the flood came and took them all away**... Matt. 24:37-39a*

Isaiah (Isaiah 54:9), Ezekiel (Ezekiel 14:14), and Peter (2Peter 2:5) also all mention a literal flood over the entire earth.

...the unbelieving world doesn't accept that the Bible is God's infallible word-for-word truth.

But the unbelieving world doesn't accept that the Bible is God's infallible word-for-word truth. Most non-Believers think the creation story, the worldwide flood, the account of Jonah and the great fish, etc., are fanciful, imaginative, and made-up stories.

They SHOULD be concerned because if they can't shout down the truth about the accuracy of the story of Noah, then other parts of the Bible might also be true—like heaven and hell and who goes where. So they call Christians everything from "idiots" to "ignoring science."

Their arguments really sound more like accusations because, again, if they lose this argument, oh dear, the Bible may be true. And that, of course, is unacceptable to have to be accountable to a sovereign and righteous God.

So then each one of us will give an account of himself to God. Rom. 14:12

So their annoyance will move to anger and then to furious wrath. We should expect it. In fact, the Bible says that in the time in which we live there will be mockers mocking. And they will vocally deride both Noah's worldwide flood and the Second Coming.

> ***...in the last days mockers will come...***

*Know this first of all, that **in the last days mockers will come** with their mocking, following after their own lusts, and saying, **"Where is the promise of His coming?** For ever since the fathers fell asleep, all continues just as it was from the beginning of creation. For when they maintain this, it escapes their notice that by the word of God the heavens existed long ago and the earth was formed out of water and by water, through which **the world at that time was destroyed, being flooded with water.** 2Pet. 3:3-6*

Therefore, to provide some armor to use when this discussion comes up with friends, family, and coworkers, here are some basic answers to a few of the typical arguments against Noah building an Ark and surviving a horrific and catastrophic flood of the earth.

The Bible says the flood was worldwide.

*The water prevailed more and more upon the earth,
so that all the high mountains everywhere under the
heavens were covered. Gen. 7:19*

Bible skeptics say: "Obviously the flood had to be local
and not worldwide because it could not have covered all
the mountain peaks like Mt. Everest."

Answer: This is the classic mistake of wrong assump-
tions. They're assuming that the mountains like Mt. Everest were the same height prior to the flood. But they were
not.

Things were dramatically different before the flood as
God created the earth perfectly. It didn't even rain before
the flood... which I'm sure made Noah and his family the
laughing stock of earth at the time he spent his whole life
and all his money building the Ark.

Below in Psalm 104:6-9 you can plainly see that after the
world was flooded, THEN the mountains were raised and
the valleys created by God. So the water only had to cover
the highest mountain at the time of Noah.

*You covered it with the deep as with a garment; **The waters were standing above the mountains.** At Your re-
buke they fled, at the sound of Your thunder they hurried
away. **The mountains rose; the valleys sank down** to
the place which you established for them. Ps. 104:6-9*

Scientists now have discovered there is a lot more water below the surface than above. Therefore there's certainly plenty of water to flood the earth from below.

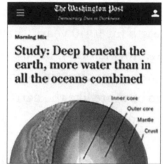

It's a fact that there's enough water on the exterior of the earth today that if the earth was smoothed over, the mountains flattened and the ocean depths raised, the water would be two miles deep over the entire earth!

It's also worth noting that the reason we have bad weather today is because when God "raised the mountains and lowered the valleys," the height and topography of these NEW mountains caused the storms, tornadoes, flooding, hurricanes, tsunamis, and such that we have today.

And even more interestingly, during the coming Seven-Year Tribulation, the Bible says the mountains will again be lowered due to God shaking the earth.

*...And the earth will be **shaken** from its place. Isa. 13:13*

*...The earth is **shaken violently**. Isa. 24:19*

And every island fled away, and the mountains were not found. Rev. 16:20

Therefore, after the tribulation when Jesus reigns on the earth for 1000 years, there won't be weather problems with which He'll have to concern Himself. The removal of the high mountains will smooth down the earth's surface to be more like the earth before the flood when there were no storms.

There's no telling how beautiful the earth was prior to the flood. The residual beauty today is probably only slightly similar to the unimaginable lushness of original earth created by God. All we know is that the destructive flood and receding waters radically rearranged the earth's surface.

The flood lasted for more than a year so there is no way it was a local flood, it could only be global. And if it was local, there would have been no need for an Ark to save mankind and all the animals.

Trying to make it local undermines the specificity of the account in the Bible, making a mockery of Scripture.

The Bible says EVERYTHING was destroyed by the flood.

*Thus **He blotted out every living thing** that was upon the face of the land, from man to animals to creeping things and to birds of the sky, and they were blotted out from the earth; and only Noah was left, together with those that were with him in the ark. Gen. 7:23*

Bible skeptics say: "Why would God flood the earth when he could just 'poof' everyone out of existence? That's so inefficient."

Answer: God is God, He can do what He wants. He makes the rules and didn't consult us humans. He defines sin and the penalties for unforgiven sin. What He does, according to the Bible, is in our best interest, even if we don't understand it.

> *For My thoughts are not your thoughts, nor are your ways My ways, declares the LORD. Isa 55:8*

The Bible says the earth was destroyed by water:

> *Behold, I, even I am bringing the flood of water upon the earth, to destroy all flesh in which is the breath of life, from under heaven; everything that is on the earth shall perish. Gen. 6:17*

Bible skeptics say: "There is no geographical or archaeological evidence whatsoever for a worldwide flood."

Answer: <u>That is simply not true.</u> The evidence for a worldwide flood is overwhelming. If there was a catastrophic worldwide flood where much or most of the water came from below, you would expect to find layers of sedimentary rock laid down quickly by water containing billions of dead things/fossils all over the earth.

And that's exactly what we find today—billions of fossils of plants and animal fossils laid down in sedimentary layers all over the globe. They were drowned and buried so quickly they couldn't even be eaten by scavengers.

And to add cold water in the face of evolutionists, the layers of sedimentary layers all over the globe are laid down by weight, the heaviest material sank first to the bottom and the lightest sank last and is at the top — perfectly graduated by weight. Exactly what you would expect from a worldwide flood.

Fish Fossils Above 10,000 Feet

Millions of fish died in the turbulent waters during the

flood and are fossilized today for us to see. Below is a fish fossil that not only contains a fossilized fish but also fish feces near his mouth.

When a fish poops in the water, the feces disintegrates in about 20-30 seconds. So for the fish to have been cov- ered and fossilized together with its poop, it would have had to have been a quite-sudden and catastrophic event.

Even more interesting is that the fish and poop fossil was found near the top of Mt. Evans in Colorado, one of the highest mountains in Colorado at over 14,000 feet in ele- vation. How did those fish get buried quickly up that high if there had been no worldwide flood covering the moun- tains? Why can fish fossils be found on or near the top of every mountain worldwide? **Because the flood covered the whole earth!**

The Bible says the Ark held two of every kind of animal.

You shall take with you of every clean animal by sevens, a male and his female; and of the animals that are not clean two, a male and his female... Gen. 7:2

Bible skeptics say: There is no way two of all the ani- mals on the earth could fit in the Ark!

Answer: That's precisely why the rebuilt Noah's Ark in Kentucky is raising so many eyebrows. It proves that the Ark, built to the dimensions God gave Noah in Genesis, is large enough to contain two of every **kind** (not species) of animal in the world. And plenty of room left over for Noah and his family and food and water for all to live for over a year—with room to spare!

The rebuilt Ark in Kentucky even shows how Noah's family would have been able to care for all the animals and dispose of all their waste. It is likely Noah and his family had to deal with only about 6700 individual animals, and most of them were small and easily maintained.

Dinosaurs are often brought up for ridicule due to their size. But only two dinosaurs would have been needed, and most dinosaurs were about the size of an average sheep. Not to mention, you didn't need to bring along adults of every "kind," two youths of each kind would do. You didn't need one of every dog breed. Two dogs would do just fine.

Skeptics love to press the question, "You're telling me all the dog breeds in the world came from only two dogs?"

And of course the answer is yes, and it is easily proven through genetics. But also it's fun to point out they think that dogs evolved from a rock!

———

The Bible says God gathered the animals and birds to the Ark.

Of the birds after their kind, and of the animals after their kind, of every creeping thing of the ground after its kind, two of every kind will come to you to keep them alive. Gen. 6:20

... went into the ark to Noah by twos, male and female, as God had commanded Noah. Gen. 7:9

Bible skeptics say: How did all the animals get to the Ark from other continents?

Answer: The Bible says God brought the animals. He certainly could have supernaturally brought them from afar. But also it's possible that there was just one continent at the time on the earth.

———

The Bible says God gave the size of the Ark to build.

"This is how you shall make it: the length of the ark three hundred cubits, its breadth fifty cubits, and its height thirty cubits." Gen. 6:15 (over 500 feet long)

Bible skeptics say: "Noah didn't have the technology or manpower to build a boat of that size."

Answer: The Ark was built only 16 centuries from the time of Adam, and humans were originally built perfectly. The ravages of sin had only begun to take its toll. The Bible says they were building cities, making musical instruments, and even working with metal (Genesis 4:17, 21, 22). So there's no reason to think that Noah couldn't have built the Ark.

The Bible doesn't say whether Noah employed outside personnel to assist in the construction, which is possible. But even if the Ark construction was limited to Noah and his sons, they had ample time to build the Ark... between 80 and 100 years.

...we need to never forget the reason for Noah's Flood...

It's not surprising that the God-ordained ratio of 300 X 50 X 30 is the standard ratio used in shipbuilding today as it is known to be the most seaworthy.

The Bible says God destroyed every living thing in the flood.

Behold, I, even I am bringing the flood of water upon the earth, to destroy all flesh in which is the breath of life, from under heaven; everything that is on the earth shall perish. Gen. 6:17

Bible skeptics say: A loving God would never destroy so many innocent people.

Answer: Not true. God is a God of justice and sometimes killed tens of thousands of people at a time in the Old Testament due to mankind's sinful ways. Thankfully He sent His only Son to pay the price for our sins so we could escape the penalty of eternal death. This free gift is open to anyone who believes the Gospel.

> *"God gives us an account of His past judgments to remind us of His future prophesied judgments." BP*

> *...if you confess with your mouth Jesus as Lord, and believe in your heart that God raised Him from the dead, you will be saved... Rom. 10:9*

Why?

And we need to never forget **THE REASON** for Noah's Flood: **God's worldwide judgment on a sinful people.** Our loving God is a righteous but just God. God gives us an account of His past judgments to remind us of his future prophesied judgments. God is not mocked.

There is a penalty for sin. And there is a future worldwide judgment coming after the Lord removes His Holy Spirit from the earth, along with those in whom His Spirit dwells. The Flood of Noah is a reminder of that fact.

CHAPTER FOUR

ISRAEL'S COMING MIND-BLOWING GOLD RICHES
And Russia's Evil Plan to Steal It

.... *"Have you [Gog/Russia] come to capture spoil? Have you assembled your company to seize plunder, to carry away **silver** and **gold**, to take away cattle and goods, to capture **great spoil**?" Ezek. 38:13*

How much gold and silver would it take for Russia to be enticed to invade Israel to steal it all? A bunch. It would have to be a tantalizing amount, probably in the billions, if not trillions, of dollars.

But even if Israel were to discover a mega hoard of gold and silver, enough to entice the Russians, the timing of such an invasion (basically starting World War III) would have to be seen as the "perfect window of opportunity."

Well, the Bible says Russia, Iran and others WILL invade Israel to steal her gold and silver, and this future invasion is described in Ezekiel 38 and 39... a fascinating read. And a great "opportunity window" will open for the Russians to make their move during the 50 chaotic days between Rapture and the signing of the 10-Nation Peace Treaty.[1]

Think about it—the United States is Israel's only true ally, and the U.S. will be decimated from the effects of losing key people in the sudden Rapture. So Israel will be alone in the world to fend for herself.

God comes to Israel's help in a mighty way to supernaturally protect Israel.

At least that's what the Russians will think. They will conclude they can invade and capture the vast treasure for themselves. But God comes to Israel's help in a mighty way to supernaturally protect Israel. And Russia goes down in an embarrassing defeat.[2]

Are the riches future oil discoveries? Nope!

So, if we're as close as I think we are to the Rapture, where is this great treasure that Russia will be trying to capture? For years I must admit I thought the treasure would be Israel striking huge amounts of oil. And indeed they have struck a great quantity of oil and gas.

But thinking about that reasoning, Saudi Arabia has a lot more oil with far fewer national defenses and I don't see Russia going after Saudis' oil.

Massive amounts of gold and silver? Yes!

And now, as I've reread the text of Ezekiel 38:13, I realize I was wrong. It's not oil. The Bible specifically says Russia comes after "silver and gold." I'm quite humbled that I missed that! However, there's a problem. At the moment, Israel doesn't have vast amounts of gold and silver. She does have a great diamond-cutting business, world renown. But they just cut other people's diamonds.

So how in the world could Israel end up with enough gold and silver to entice Russia to invade? Well, as it turns out, the Bible says that amount of gold and silver treasure is already in Israel, they just need to find it—quite interesting, huh?

Hang with me as I back up a bit...

Solomon was the richest man in the world, literally. His treasures were unfathomable. God gave him his wealth because he wisely asked for wisdom, not riches, but God rewarded him for his humble answer and gave him both wisdom AND wealth...great wealth (1Kings 3:9-13).

The Bible, and even 1st century Jewish historian Josephus, mentions that Solomon had a fleet of ships that did business all over the Mediterranean. And each time the fleet returned to Israel they brought the trip's profit in gold to King Solomon.

> *...the Bible says that amount of gold and silver treasure is already in Israel, they just need to find it...*

Just how rich WAS Solomon?

Solomon had dominion over everything from west of the

Jordan River to the Egyptian border in the south and north into present-day Syria. And God allowed him to be at peace with the surrounding nations (1Kings 4:24). He was in the perfect place to make tons of money.

In 1Kings 9:26-28, it records that a fleet of his ships returned to Israel with a profit of 31,500 pounds of gold! That's close to a trillion dollars in today's value. And that was from just one sea-faring business trip abroad.

In 1Kings 10 it says the Queen of Sheba came to Israel to pay Solomon a visit to hear his wisdom and see his wealth. She was stunned—so impressed that she was moved to give Solomon over $200 million in gold plus untold numbers of precious stones. The amount of gold and silver that Solomon acquired during his kingship was beyond imagination, as you will soon see.

Solomon builds the 1st Jewish Temple

In 970 BC, Solomon built the first Jewish Temple to be a permanent replacement for the Tabernacle that had been carted around the Middle East for hundreds of years. The Scriptures outlining the building of the Temple make a good outline for a business plan, in writing, dealing with planning, labor, and materials management (1Chronicles 28; 1Kings 5,6).

Solomon was so rich when he built the Temple that, rather than putting in just one solid gold menorah, he decided to multiply the contents on the inside of the Temple by 10.

So Solomon made nine more solid gold menorahs and lined up the 10 in two rows of five each (2Chronicles 4:7,8). This means there were 10 six-foot-high solid gold menorahs in the 1st Jewish Temple. (See drawing above of the inside of the 1st Temple made by the Temple Institute in Jerusalem.)

Each of those solid gold menorahs was so heavy that the Temple priests estimated their value at $360 billion each, $2.5 trillion value for all 10!

Solomon also increased from having one solid-gold Table of Showbread inside the Temple to 10. Each of these solid gold tables held twelve loaves of bread. The Temple Institute says they would have been about six feet high, four feet wide and four feet long. (See the drawing, right.) That's a lot of gold. And a lot of bread to bake daily.

We don't know how much the Tables of Showbread

weighed—they had to each hold only 12 loaves of bread—but they still were solid gold.

However, if they weighed 1/4 of the menorahs, that's another $500 billion in value for the 10 tables. And this doesn't include all the golden bowls, plates, and such that numbered in the thousands.

> *But with all that success, Israel got her eyes off the Lord.*

Again, Solomon could afford to make all this because he had unfathomable riches. His wealth of gold, silver, precious stones, and other things became legendary. So much so that ultimately Israel became a target for conquest by surrounding nations.

The king made silver and gold as plentiful in Jerusalem as stones... 2Chr. 1:15a

But with all that success, Israel got her eyes off the Lord. Eventually Solomon brought in hundreds of foreign wives and concubines to pleasure himself. And 40 years later, in 930 BC, Israel split into North and South.

In the North, Israel set up its own sacrificial system. But sacrifices could be made only on Mt. Moriah in Jerusalem, and breaking that rule meant they were the first to be conquered. The Assyrians were God's war-club, allowing Israel's Northern 10 tribes to be conquered in 721 BC.

But Assyria was unable to capture the real prize—Jerusalem/Judah in the South with all her riches.

The South, Judah, held on for over a hundred years, but finally Jerusalem was conquered by Nebuchadnezzar's armies in 586 BC. History tells us that Nebuchadnezzar, King of Babylon, plundered the Temple and deported Jerusalem's wealthy and educated inhabitants to Babylon.

They looted what they found in the Temple. But apparently Israel had thrown them a bone, leaving what seemed like a great treasure to find and seize, but it was actually only a fraction of the massive treasure trove, only about 2% of the total.

The 5,400 items that were captured were eventually returned by Cyrus, King of Persia, when he authorized their rebuilding of the Temple after Israel's 70 years of Babylonian Captivity. The Bible is clear that Cyrus returned all that had been stolen, even listing out the items (Ezra 1:5-11).

The Bible is clear that Cyrus returned all that had been stolen...

But none of the 10 solid gold menorahs were mentioned or any tables of showbread on Cyrus' list (Ezra 1:9-11). Nor was there any mention of the other tens of thousands of gold and silver Temple implements or gold and silver bars from the treasury.

What happened to the Temple treasures?

Now, since only a small fraction of all that gold and silver went to Babylon, what happened to the other 98%? Basically we're missing the entire fortune that Israel had accumulated under Solomon—trillions of dollars in silver and gold!

What happened to the other 98%?

In the Jewish Talmud, tradition says that King Josiah and the Temple priests hid the vast treasure, including the Ark of the Covenant, in secret winding passages under the Temple Mount 10 years before the 1st Temple's destruction.

Well, the Jews are a smart people, and Israel did have 140+ years to think about what to do if Jerusalem was ever conquered like their brothers in the north. And Zechariah, God's prophet of the day, was continually hammering the Israelites to wake up and clean up their sins or the Lord would allow them to be conquered like their Northern brothers.

Zechariah, unlike most other prophets, was also a priest. He knew it was possible that Israel was going to be conquered. And he would have had first-hand knowledge of the vast riches stored in the Temple treasuries. He was in the unique position to approve plans to hide the treasure if it looked imminent that Israel would be conquered, fulfilling his own prophetic predictions.

Zechariah would certainly want to protect as much of Israel's riches as he could, including those 10 golden menorahs and 10 golden Tables of Showbread. Not to mention the hugely important Holy Ark of the Covenant that contained Moses'/Aaron's staff and the two stone tablets with the 10 Commandments.

So apparently Zechariah approved the hiding/burying of the Temple treasures. And Israel was smart enough to throw the Babylonians a bone. They left in the Temple several thousand gold and silver utensils, which would normally be significant spoils of war.

The ruse worked. History tells us that Nebuchadnezzar plundered what they found in the Temple and deported Jerusalem's upper-class citizens, like Daniel, to Babylon.

However, Zechariah hid the rest of the treasure so well it's never been found to this day.

Qumran and the Copper Scroll

Since 1947, in and around Qumran down by the Dead Sea, thousands of pieces of parchment were found buried in caves in the cliffs surrounding the area.

Collectively called the Dead Sea Scrolls, their discovery came within months of Israel becoming a fledgling nation again, and Jews today readily admit the discovery helped awaken Jews around the world to their Biblical roots.

But in 1952 another scroll was found, one made not of parchment but of copper mixed with a tiny bit of tin.

This Copper Scroll wasn't found near any of the parchment scrolls, but rather by itself, on a carved-out shelf in the back of a cave near the area of Qumran.

Since it was written on copper, whoever wrote it thought the contents so valuable they had to make permanent indentations in metal to stand the test of time.

All the other Dead Sea Scrolls contained Old Testament books, Scripture commentaries, and general Jewish life observations. But the Copper Scroll was simply a list of instructions of where to find where the tons of gold, silver, and precious stones were buried, along with a lengthy list of gold and silver items.

COLUMN X OF THE COPPER SCROLL

But, as Frank Peretti said in his classic THE CHAIR presentation, you have to have a "fixed point of reference" to know where to begin any journey. And there are no reference points in the Copper Scroll instructions, so they don't know where to begin to look.

Though many have tried, no one yet has been able to figure out the right place to dig. Probably they were written vaguely on purpose because once they find just one of the 64 locations, they'll be able find the rest of the massive treasure.

Biblical archaeologists who've analyzed the Copper Scroll believe it to be written by five different people who apparently were in a major hurry to complete the scroll.

Hebrew priests normally take great care in making each line perfect, but the Copper Scroll looks as if time was of the essence to complete it. Lines are not uniform, some letters are hard to read, there are misspellings, etc.

In 1952 another scroll was found...

The Copper Scroll is most fascinating because 63 of the 64 locations described listed staggering quantities of gold and silver. There are even some large unnamed items that very well could be the 10 missing 1st Temple menorahs and Tables of Showbread.

In total, there were over 345,000 pounds of gold and silver listed, not counting the 10 menorahs and 10 Tables of Showbread. That's over $5 trillion in today's U.S dollar! Certainly enough to entice the Russians to "devise an evil plan." (Ezekiel 38:10)

But, as the commercials always say, "That's not all!"

More to the story...

2Maccabees 2:1 (granted, it's not part of inspired Hebrew Scripture but heavily relied on and quoted by Jewish historians) mentions that Jeremiah, another of God's prophets at the same time as Zechariah, made records of the Temple inventory. He even warned those helping him make the records not to be "led astray in their thoughts upon seeing all the gold and silver."

The Maccabean text continues to say that Jeremiah then found a cave to store the treasure, including the Ark of the Covenant, and covered up the entrance saying the treasure would not be found until "God gathers His people together and shows His mercy."

Several have spent small fortunes looking for these Temple treasures...

Over the last 75 years, several Americans have raised and spent small fortunes looking for these Temple treasures in Israel. Most notably, John Allegro, Vendyl Jones, Oren Gutfield, and Jim Barfield.

Others, like Randall Price, go on yearly digs to find anything they can. So the area will eventually yield its fruit.

In the meantime, with each failure of discovery, the chorus of naysayers who don't believe the treasure is real grows louder and louder. But all that gold and silver is hiding somewhere and will one day be found.

A Most Intriguing List

Several hundred years ago, some Hebrew scholars decided to try to locate these "other records" that Jeremiah mentioned. They found what they were looking for in the *Emeq HaMelekh,* which means "Valley of the Kings."

In 1648, a rabbi translated *Emeq HaMelekh,* and his translations were discovered in 1992.

Emeq HaMelekh is a Hebrew account of five Temple guardians who hid the Ark of the Covenant, the Sanctuary, and the Treasures of Solomon's Temple. Could those five be the same five guys on the Copper Scroll? Very plausible, to say the least!

Most importantly to this chapter, the *Emeq HaMelekh* has a lot in common with the Copper Scroll list of Temple treasures, but it lists about 100 times more pieces of gold and silver. Now we're easily into the quadrillions of dollars worth of gold and silver waiting to be discovered.

To save space, I have made an edited (but numerically accurate) recap of the *Emeq HaMelekh*. I have added notes in bold italics, including calculated amounts in today's dollars on some of the items to give you a feel for how much it is. [Note: A talent was approximately 75 lbs.]

* * *

Emeq HaMelekh

These are the vessels dedicated and concealed when the Temple was destroyed:

Mishnah 1

- The Tabernacle and the Curtain
- The Holy Menorah
- The Ark of the Testimony
- The golden forehead Nameplate
- The golden crown of Aharon the Cohen
- The Breastplate of Judgment
- The silver Trumpets
- The Cherubim
- The Altar of burnt offerings
- The curtain of the Communion Tent
- The forks and the bread molds
- The Table of Showbread

[The list "Mishnah 1" continues with several pages of priestly only garments that are not included here.]

Mishnah 2

These are the holy vessels and the vessels of the Temple that were in Jerusalem and in every place. They were inscribed by Shimur Halevi and his companions on a Luach

Nehoshef Copper Plate with all the Vessels of the Holy of Holies that Shlomo son of David made. And together with Shimur were Hizkiyahu, Zidkiyah, Haggai the Prophet, and Zechariah, son of Berachiah, son of Iddo the Prophet.

Mishnah 3

These are the components and vessels of the Temple that were taken and buried in the ground:

- The locking rods
- The pegs
- The boards
- The rings
- The standing pillars of the courtyard

These are the Vessels:

- 1,200,000 silver Mizrakot (sacrificial basins)
- 50,000 fine gold Mizrakot (sacrificial basins)
- 600,000 bowls of fine gold
- 1,200,000 bowls of silver

Mishnah 4

- 500,000 trays of fine gold
- 1,200,000 trays of silver
- 500,000 bread molds of fine gold
- 1,200,000 bread molds of silver

[Calculations in italics added for reference. Gold figured at $1500 per once.]

On each of the molds there were five Margallot/pearls and two precious gem stones. The value of each precious stone was 100 talents of gold *($180 million)*. The total value of all the Margallot was 200,000 talents of gold *($360 billion)*.

- 36 golden trumpets
- 7-branched menorah of fine gold worth 100,000 talents *($180 billion)*

Mishnah 5

- 77 tables of gold
- 7,000 talents of gold *($12 billion)*
- 3 rows of priceless stones, 7 cubits by 5 cubits

Mishnah 7

The counting of precious stones, Margallot gems, silver, and gold that King David dedicated to the great Temple was:
- 1,000,000 talents of silver *($36 billion)*
- 100,000 talents of gold *($360 billion)*
- 600,000 talents of fine gold *($2.2 trillion—see graphic below)*

talents of gold	lbs	total pounds	oz	ounces	per ounce	Total value
600,000	75	45,000,000	32	1,440,000,000	1500	$2,160,000,000,000

All these were concealed, hidden, and safeguarded from the army of the Chaldeans in a place called Borseef.

Mishnah 8

- 7 golden curtains with 12,000 talents of gold *($20B)*
- 12,000 Levitical garments with belts

- 70,000 Levitical garments with belts, turbans, and pants

All of these service clothes were concealed until the future to atone for Israel in the end of days.

Mishnah 9

David also made:
- 1,000 copper lyres overlaid with fine gold and 8 stones
- 7,000 harps

All these were hidden and concealed in Ein Zidkiyah that the fittest men of Israel knew in secret, lest they fall, G-d forbid, into the hands of the enemy who hated Israel.

These vessels are not to be used except to atone for Israel, thus concealed to prevent the Chaldeans from using them, G-d forbid.

They hid them until the day when Israel will return to their former stature and reclaim eternal honor and worldly glory, and they find a man named David, son of David. The silver and gold shall then be unearthed to him, when all Israel shall gather and make a complete Aliyah ascent to Jerusalem. Amen.

Mishnah 10

These are the weights of silver concealed at Ein Kahal by Baruch and Zidkiyah:

- 1,200,000 talents of silver *($43 billion)*
- 1,600,000 talents of fine silver *($57 billion)*
- 2,000,000 pots of fine copper
- 1,100,000 pots of iron
- 3,000 frying pans of fine gold *(LOL!)*
- Countless copper sinks and lavers
- 70 tables of fine gold

All those were concealed by Zidkiyah.

Mishnah 11

Treasures of gold and silver stored away from the days of David until Zidkiyah and until Israel was exiled to Babylon.

- Hundreds of thousands of golden shields
- Countless silver shields
- 353,000 precious stones
- 1,900,000 Korin of gold *[no clue what that weighs]*

All the prophets, wise men, and scribes in the world could not calculate the wealth and the glory that was in Jerusalem.

Mishnah 12

Twelve precious stones with the names of the Tribes engraved on them.

No king, prophet, or anyone else knew where they were hidden, excepting Hiluk, son of Shimur Halevi.

All Israel concealed the Vessels until a righteous king arises over Israel. What's more, they all share a solemn vow never to reveal the whereabouts of these vessels until David, son of David, arises.

All silver, gold, and Margallot precious stones which were ever hidden away will be handed over to him when the exiles of Israel will be gathered from the four ends of the earth, and they ascend with greatness and exaltation to the land of Israel. At that time a great river will issue forth from the Holy of Holies of the Temple. Its name is Gihon and it will flow to the great and dreadful desert and become mixed with the Euphrates River.

* * *

Well, there you have it—Trillions of dollars of gold and silver are still hidden somewhere in Israel. Not to mention all those 3,000 gold frying pans! Certainly enough to entice Russia to invade if they see a window of opportunity.

And when Israel does find that incredible treasure, look up!

But when these things begin to take place, straighten up and lift up your heads, because your redemption is drawing near. Lk. 21:28

References:
1) https://compass.org/article-the-50-days-between-rapture-and-the-great-tribulation/
2) https://compass.org/article-russias-humiliating-defeat/

CHAPTER FIVE

BEHEADINGS AND THE BIBLE

DEFEAT OR BE DEFEATED

The cold-hearted murders by Muslims in Paris in January 2015 finally exposed to the world what we're actually dealing with in respect to Islamic ideals and goals. Their goal is simple: They fully expect and work toward the world becoming 100% Islamic under Shari'ah Law.

You can laugh at Islam's world domination agenda if you want, but this clash of values will continue worldwide until either the Muslims are in full control or they are defeated. Yes, defeated. **They will defeat us or we will defeat them.** And if we don't begin to think in those terms, we will lose.

Over 100 Syrians, dozens of Lebanese soldiers, 10 Kurds, two American journalists, and three American and British aid workers were **beheaded** by the Islamic State in 2015. These were not war kills, but rather mostly innocent humans who were murdered as a sort of appeasement to Allah.

Europe is in a mess!

There are some 50 million Muslims living legally or illegally in Europe today, steadfastly refusing to assimilate into the local culture. The liberal European governments, until recently, left the Muslims to themselves.

Europe	
% of population Muslim	
1. Marseille	30%
2. Brussels	25%
3. Rotterdam	25%
4. Amsterdam	24%
5. Paris	15%
6. London	12%

Unfortunately, inaction is not what is needed. By not addressing the true problem from the beginning, the Muslim population in Europe has now grown to be pretty much unmanageable.

Consider Belgium

For at least four years in a row, the number one baby name was "Mohammad." Forty percent of the school children were Muslim. And the Muslims won't assimilate into the Belgian culture, instead remaining segregated and using their own schools and Shari'ah courts.

Now even Japan

Wanting to equally offend the world, in 2015 the Muslims announced they had two Japanese men in custody and demanded some $100 million or they would be **beheaded**.

What's Really Happening

As the Church Age draws closer to its exciting conclusion for Believers, God is setting the stage for the Tribulation events to begin. We  can see in the Bible that all but one country (Russia) who comes against Israel in the Tribulation is Islamic.

And it's fascinating to read that in the Tribulation, **a large number of those who die standing on their belief in Jesus are actually beheaded.**

An uncountable number of deaths in the Tribulation are due to faith in Jesus (Revelation 7:9-14), and it's most interesting that "beheading" is the only murder specifically described.

So what we're seeing take place in the world today is simply a prelude to the satanic wars of the Tribulation when **beheadings will be quite common** for the uncountable millions who follow Jesus.

So much so that those of us in heaven will be crying out, "How much longer?" (Revelation 6:9-11)

Rev 20:4 ...And I saw the souls of those who had been beheaded because of their testimony of Jesus and because of the word of God, and those who had not worshiped the beast or his image, and had not received the mark on their forehead and on their hand;

Setting the Stage

While the West has been for decades buying Satan's lie by actively declining God's blessing of children (via birth control, abortion, and other non-God-centered priorities), the Muslim population is multiplying at four to five times the rate of natives in the countries to which they've immigrated.

The FACT is, it's only a matter of time before they can just VOTE themselves into control of governments.

But they're not just waiting to have enough babies to get their way. They now have enough population currently in place in Europe to begin brazenly exerting their power. France and Belgium are just the first to see the Muslims' true intents.

Look at History

In the 6th century AD, it seems as though Satan saw the need to blunt the early church's explosive growth so he used Muhammad and Islam as his tool.

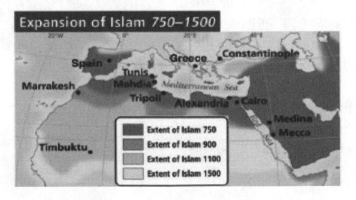

Since 600 AD, Islam grew east and west. With the exception of the Crusader Period for a brief time around 1100 AD, the Muslims basically spread unchecked. And by the **1500s, they reached so far as to control all of Spain, Portugal, and Greece**!

Christianity is spread through sharing the Good News of a loving God Who sent His Son as Savior, paying for our sins and promising eternal life to all who simply "Believe."

But in Islam there is no promise of salvation. The Muslim believes that when he or she dies, they stand before Allah to have life's deeds judged, hoping he allows them into Paradise. The lone exception is through martyrdom, where the martyr not only is promised heaven with 72 virgins, he could also bring with him 72 members of his family.

This is not a sick joke. This is quite appealing to the typical martyr—a Muslim male between the age of 18 and 35 who has no assets, no job, and no future. The promise of going to heaven (referred to as "Paradise" by Islam) as a hero to his family is expertly fanned by Satan's minions.

> *The Messenger of Allah said: "I have been commanded to fight against the people till they testify that there is no god but Allah, that Muhammad is the messenger of Allah." (Muslim Hadith 1:33)*

And with over **100 verses in the Koran that say to murder the Jews and/or Christians**, it's easy to push those Satanically blinded youth into doing what is unthinkable to any non-Muslim.

America's First War was against... guess who?

So Islam has spread through the fear of an unloving, unforgiving god who requires strict obedience to the Koran. Those who didn't convert had the choice of paying "tribute" or bribes or were killed by beheading. Imagine going on one of their mission trips! "Worship Allah or we will kill you!"

We shake our heads at the tactics, but it's been hugely successful for 1400 years! Most Americans think our first war after gaining independence was in 1812 against Britain. But that's not true. After our war for independence from 1776-1784, **our first war was actually against the Muslims**!

When we began as a nation in the late 1700s, along with the rest of the civilized world we paid tribute (bribes) to the Muslims of North Africa to not attack our merchant ships in the Mediterranean Sea.

Only when Thomas Jefferson was elected President in 1801 did we cease paying these bribes.

Tomas Jefferson

Interestingly, Jefferson didn't just stop paying bribes. After reading what was written in the Koran, he also sent a fleet of American ships to bomb the smithereens out of the North African coastal harbors of Tunis, Algiers, and Tripoli. Only after repeated pummeling by the Americans did they agree to allow our ships safe passage.

Which brings up a major point

We learned from Israel that you can't negotiate fairly with a Muslim because the Bible says they are born irrational. You value life, they don't. And they're predisposed to fighting anyone and everyone. (Genesis 16:12)

You may think you're negotiating, but they simply lie about their intentions, and they love to fight...which is irrational. If you don't knock them in the head, they won't get it.

Israel, surrounded by their Muslim enemies, has found this out the hard way. **Most Muslims countries have a long history of breaking treaties.**

The only thing Muslims truly understand is pain and consequence. Muslims only wave the white flag if the pain is so great they think they will lose the battle. But surrender is only to delay until they attack again later.

Israel exists today because they inflict enormous pain in response to all acts of Muslim terrorism. And they certainly don't trust the Muslims for their safety. Imagine if the Muslims had a nuclear bomb...how long before they would use it on Israel? Or the West? Two seconds.

Muslims are to "behead" foes

But why in the world do Muslims behead their enemies? That seems to us quite archaic. But there is a simple answer. The Koran, their bible, **calls for beheading their enemies**.

I will cast terror into the hearts of those who disbelieve...

So when you meet those who disbelieve, strike their necks until you have inflicted slaughter upon them... Surah 47:4

"I will cast terror into the hearts of those who disbelieve, so strike them upon the necks...." Surah 8:12

So they behead because Allah says to behead. You have to keep reminding yourself who Allah really represents for this to make any sense.

Beheadings in the Tribulation

The Bible also tells us where all this will culminate. After the Church Age ends, the Bible specifically mentions "beheadings" as a major way Believers die in the future Seven-Year Tribulation.

That's amazing since we're starting to often actually see the Muslims beheading people around the world.

And they're the only ones doing that barbaric act. So, if we're close to the end of the Church Age, we can easily project who the bad guys are in the Tribulation that follows.

It'll be Satan, using the Muslims, against God's Israel. Thankfully we know who wins. And thankfully we'll not be here to personally experience the shear horror of all those heads rolling.

And until the Rapture, what we MUST DO is **be wise and aware** as God allows all these things to come together for His purposes. And be willingly used by Him to witness His True Agape Love as He opens doors of opportunity.

And certainly do pray for our country's protection because it's no longer hoping our kids and grandkids will have the same lifestyle we've had, **it's now our kids' and grandkids' freedom that's at stake!**

Our mostly Christian founders fought for these privileges:

- Freedom of religion.
- Freedom of speech.
- Freedom of assembly.
- Freedom of the press.
- Freedom of addressing grievances.

None of these are allowed under Islam! Wake up, America! None of these are allowed under Communism either! And socialism is the last step before Communism.

CHAPTER SIX

TWO DAYS IN SCRIPTURE

An amazing chart that unlocks a hidden Biblical truth!

When God created the world in six literal 24-hour days and rested on the seventh, He gave us an incredible template of time He designated for the earth. This seven-day creation/rest template is hugely valuable in seeing where we've been and where we're headed.

The concept is really very simple—on the first four days of creation, no life was created. Life was created on days 5 and 6. And God rested on the seventh 24-hour day. So the template is four days without life, two days with life, and one day of rest.

God's Creation Model for Time

Day 1	Day 2	Day 3	Day 4	Day 5	Day 6	Day 7
Light	Heavens	Land	Sun	Life	Life	Rest

←———————— 4 ————————→ ←——— 2 ———→ ←— 1 —→

† Today   Tomorrow   Third Day

1000	1000	1000	1000	1000	1000	1000
No Life	No Life	No Life	No Life	Life	Life	Rest

Now to God, a day is "like" a thousand years. Not "is," exactly, but "like."

> But do not let this one fact escape your notice, beloved, that with the Lord **one day is** _like a thousand years_, and **a thousand years like one day.** 2Pet. 3:8

So if we take our Seven-Day Creation template and apply the "1000 years is like one day," we get a fascinating 7000-year map, or timeline model, for mankind's days on Earth. And the timeline fits like a glove.

For example, according to Ussher's chronology of the Bible, it was almost exactly 4000 years of elapsed time from Adam to when Jesus arrived, bringing "life" and the Church Age.

And we know that Jesus will reign 1000 years as King of Earth after the Church Age, which is the last day of God's timeline.

Other verses teach this. Consider this verse that only makes sense using this timeline.

> Come, let us return to the Lord. For He has torn us, but He will heal us; He has wounded us, but He will bandage us. **He will revive us after two days; He will raise us up on the third day,** that we may **live before Him.** Hos. 6:1-2

That's an unfulfilled prophecy about Israel being scattered, torn, and wounded for **two days** and then "returning"/"raised" back up on **the third day**.

But if we apply our creation model template, it translates to: God will scatter the Jews for about 2000 years before He brings them back to their homeland where they will live with their Messiah for 1000 years.

You can see this template hidden in other verses too.

*So when the Samaritans **[non-Jews]** came to Jesus, they were asking Him to stay with them; and He stayed there **two days**. Jn. 4:40*

*After the **two days** He went forth from there into Galilee. Jn. 4:43*

This is the only place the Bible records Jesus staying with non-Jews—and wouldn't you

God brings them back to their homeland where they will live with their Messiah for 1000 years.

know it, **He stayed with the non-Jews for TWO DAYS! Then He returned to the Jews.** So applying this to our template, we know that Jesus will stay with the church about 2000 years. Then He will return to making the Jews His priority.

You can also see this pattern in John 2:1, "**On the third day there was a wedding...**" After the two-day Church

Age, on the third day, the Millennium, Believers have a wedding—the Church is the Bride of Christ! This happens at the beginning of the Millennium, the third day on God's timeline.

...the Jews are to be ready for the "third day" when the Lord will "come down"...

Let us rejoice and be glad and give the glory to Him, for the marriage of the Lamb has come and His bride has made herself ready. Rev. 19:7

Here's another interesting verse:

*Jesus said, "Remove the stone." Martha, the sister of the deceased, said to Him, "Lord, by this time there will be a stench, for he has been dead **four days**." Jn. 11:39*

Lazarus was dead for four days—four days of no life—then revived on the fifth day.

And one more that'll blow your mind:

*The LORD also said to Moses, "Go to the people and consecrate them **today and tomorrow**, and let them wash their garments; and let them be ready for the third day, for on the **third day** the LORD will come down on Mount Sinai **in the sight of all the people**." Ex. 19:10-11*

"Today and tomorrow" would be referencing the two-day/2000-year Church Age, the period of time where our sins are washed away (Acts 22:16). And the Jews are to be ready for the "third day" when the Lord will "come down" from Heaven at the Second Coming and reign as King of Earth "in the sight of all." Amazing! (See chart on page 61.)

Applying this to today, Jesus died around 30 AD. So if you add two days/2,000 years, it points to this generation being quite blessed with a non-physical-death exit!

We won't know the day or the hour, but we should be able to see the equivalent of Noah loading the animals on the ark!

CHAPTER SEVEN

WAS JESUS CRUCIFIED ON FRIDAY? OR THURSDAY?

Most of the Christian world observes Jesus' death on the Friday before Resurrection Sunday. But according to the Bible, that dog won't hunt!

Most churches today teach that Friday is the day of Jesus' death on the cross. What follows is an alternate view. (I actually think I'm Biblically correct, but my wife thought I needed to soften my tone.)

First, it must be noted that the Bible gives us a detailed —VERY detailed— description of every day of Jesus' last week prior to his crucifixion. But there are only five days detailed in the Bible, instead of six. The missing day is referred to by Bible scholars as "The missing day." Not much imagination there.

It takes a lot of (guts, pride, ego, take your pick) to say there might be something left out of the Biblical narrative.

These Biblical "scholars" ASSUME that Jesus was crucified on Friday; therefore, there should be six days of details (Sunday through Friday). But only five are referenced in Scripture (Sunday through Thursday).

So most assume this is the correct calendar of the Passion Week:

- **Sunday** - Palm Sunday Road to Temple
- **Monday** - Overturned moneychangers' tables
- **Tuesday** - Priests examined Jesus
- **Wednesday** - ("Missing Day"?)
- **Thursday** - Passover preparation and meal
- **Friday** - Crucifixion, grave
- **Saturday** - Grave
- **Sunday** - Grave, Resurrection

However, if you use the above timeline, it directly contradicts this verse:

> *...for just as Jonah was **three days and three nights** in the belly of the sea monster, **so will the Son of Man be three days and three nights** in the <u>heart of the earth</u>. Matt. 12:40*

Looking at the calendar above, there's no way to get three nights between Friday afternoon and Sunday morning. The "heart of the earth" is a reference to the "bottomless pit" in the center of the earth (Revelation 9:1,2). When you are in the heart of the earth, no matter which way you look, you're looking up! After Jesus' death on the cross, He first went down to hell, the "bottomless pit," before He ascended to heaven. (1Pet. 3:18-19)

The **Old Testament** Saints could not go to heaven when they died because Jesus had yet to pay for their sins. So they went to "Paradise" to wait for their sins to be paid in full. Today, post-cross, **Church Age Believers** go straight to heaven when they die as our sins have been paid for (2Corinthians 5:8).

> *...the first thing He did was go to the Bottomless Pit to claim and release...*

Luke 16:19-31 is not a parable but rather an actual description of the bottomless pit. At death, those Old Testament saints, who trusted by faith the future Messiah's payment for sin, were enjoying paradise just a few feet from those who were wailing in the scorching flames of Hades. They were so close they could actually talk to each other across a "chasm" (v. 24-26).

It's interesting that when Jesus died and defeated death, the first thing He did was go to the Bottomless Pit to claim and release His Old Testament saints so they could go to heaven.

> *Now this expression, "He ascended," what does it mean except that He also had descended into the lower parts of the earth? He who descended is Himself also He who ascended far above all the heavens... Eph. 4:9-10*

Eighty-thousand people at a football game can make a lot of noise when someone scores, but that's nothing compared to the cheer that must have roared when Jesus made His appearance in Paradise to redeem the Old Testament saints. I'm hoping I get to see a replay of that one day!

Apparently, as the redeemed Saints crossed through the earth's crust on their way up, some lingered around and were seen by those alive on the earth.

Jesus' death paid the price of heaven's admission.

And behold, the veil of the temple was torn in two from top to bottom, and the earth shook and the rocks were split. The tombs were opened, and many bodies of the saints who had fallen asleep were raised; and **coming out of the tombs after His resurrection they entered the holy city and appeared to many.** *Matt. 27:51-53*

Having dead people walking around alive again would have really been a conversation starter at the local well! The point is, Jesus' death paid the price of heaven's admission. And Jesus spent three days **and three nights** in the heart of the earth.

So, if you ASSUME the Bible records all the events without a "missing day," using a literal translation and application of the Biblical text, you have a much more Scripturally defendable timeline:

- Sunday - Palm Sunday Road to Temple
- Monday - Overturned moneychangers' tables
- Tuesday - Priests examined Jesus
- Wednesday - Passover preparation and meal
- Thursday - Crucifixion, Grave (first night)
- Friday - Grave (second night)
- Saturday - Grave (third night)
- Sunday - Grave, Resurrection

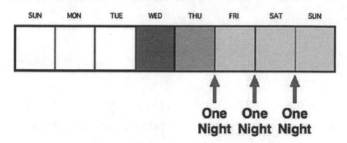

By not arbitrarily inserting the "missing day" you also solve the problem of Jesus being "three days and nights in the heart of the earth."

Any way I slice it, I can only get two nights between Friday and Sunday, even if I use a Jewish day beginning at sundown (sundown to sundown equals one day).

Therefore, the crucifixion took place on Thursday. It seems so much simpler just to follow the text as written and you have literally three days and three nights, as the Scripture says.

Now consider the verse regarding Jesus arriving at Lazarus' house.

> *Jesus, therefore, **six days before the Passover, came to Bethany** where Lazarus was, whom Jesus had raised from the dead. Jn. 12:1*

We know that the latest Jesus could have arrived at Lazarus' house would have been Friday before His Palm Sunday entry because Saturday was Shabbat and, by Jewish Law, He couldn't travel. If you count six days from Friday, you come to Thursday.

John's Gospel may also support a Thursday crucifixion:

> *Then the Jews, because it was <u>the day of preparation,</u> so that the bodies should not remain on the cross on the Sabbath (for that Sabbath was a high day)... Jn. 19:31*

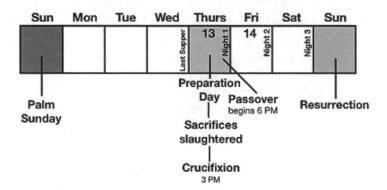

> *Then on the fourteenth day of the first month shall be the LORD'S Passover. Num. 28:16*

Passover lambs had to be slaughtered on the 13th of Nisan, the day of preparation, which was Thursday that year, 33 AD. Jesus is called the Lamb of God (John 1:29). The same time all the other Passover lambs were being sacrificed, Jesus was also being sacrificed.

So Passover would have begun on Thursday night at sundown and His disciples would have had their Passover meal on Wednesday night.

It seems so much simpler to me to just follow the text as written and you end up with literally three days and three nights—as the Scripture states!

But, of course, what's MOST important is not the day He died but the fact that He defeated death and rose from the dead.

On Sunday, three days and three nights after His crucifixion, He rose from the dead leaving his grave clothes in an empty tomb. On our Israel trips, no one ever forgets the first time they peer into that empty tomb! What an incredibly special place!

Why do you seek the living One among the dead? He is not here, but He has risen. Lk. 24:5-6

CHAPTER EIGHT

ARE THERE RESTROOMS IN HEAVEN?

I t's always fun to think about what heaven will be like. After all, the Bible does say that our glorious future life is beyond anything we can imagine.

> *...Things which eye has not seen and ear has not heard, and which have not entered the heart of man, all that God has prepared for them who love Him. 1Cor. 2:9*

We can't even imagine how good it will be. With my imagination, I can think of a lot of A+ situations to enjoy for eternity when we finally reach our heavenly goal. I look forward to being in a place with no atheists or wolves in sheep's clothing.

Yet no matter how awesome I imagine heaven could be, it's better than anything I can think of! That's amazing.

> *Yet no matter how awesome I imagine heaven could be, it's better than anything I can think of!*

We certainly won't be sitting around on clouds playing harps.

So with all my "imagination" I have some questions. For instance, what age will we be in heaven? If we live to 100, will we look old like that forever? Or will the men all look about 25 and the women 20?

Time, After Time?

Here's another question...eternity's a long time, so will we have a lot of time on our hands to fill? Will there be "time" after time? Many years ago I was taught that God is outside of time and when we get to heaven, there will be no more time. I didn't understand it but accepted it as fact.

But now as I look more closely at Scripture, it clearly says there WILL be time in heaven. Consider this verse:

> *When the Lamb broke the fifth seal, I saw underneath the altar the souls of those who had been slain because of the word of God, and because of the testimony which they had maintained; and they cried out with a loud voice, saying, "**How long**, O Lord, holy and true, will You refrain from judging and avenging our blood on those who dwell on the earth?" Rev. 6:9-10*

76

Here we see people in heaven definitely referring to time, saying "how long?" They can see the tribulation going on on the earth, not having completed its full seven years of time.

But what about the new heaven and earth? Will time stop? Clearly not!

> *But for the cowardly and unbelieving and abominable and murderers and immoral persons and sorcerers and idolaters and all liars, their part will be in **the lake that burns** with fire and brimstone, which is the second death. Rev. 21:8*

Eternity's a long time, so will we have a lot of time on our hands to fill?

Here in the New Heaven and Earth we see time mentioned regarding those who did not Believe the Gospel. They're in the "lake of fire that burns...," which is a reference to time for non-Believers who've died.

But this earth will be destroyed by fire one day at the end of the Millennium and we'll have a New Heaven and Earth (Revelation 21:1). Time will also be measured there:

> *Then he showed me a river of the water of life, clear as crystal, coming from the throne of God and of the Lamb, in the middle of its street. On either side of the river was the tree of life, bearing twelve kinds of fruit, yielding its fruit **every month** ... Rev. 22:1-2*

Every month! There won't be a sun or moon to measure time like we do today, but there's definitely "months" somehow being measured in the New Heaven and Earth.

Einstein showed that time was a physical property that varies depending on mass, acceleration, and gravity. Who knows if there's any gravity in heaven or how fast we'll be speeding through the universe.

Also, it's important to note that time on this earth, as used in our lives, was originally created "good."

> In the beginning God created the heavens and the earth.... God called the light day, and the darkness He called night. And there was evening and there was morning, one day. Gen. 1:1,5

Did Jesus go to the restroom during His 40 days on earth, post-resurrection?

> God saw all that He had made, and behold, it was very good. . . .
> Gen. 1:31

And don't miss the fact that God was referring to time being measured on Day One of the seven-day creation, prior to the sun and moon being created on Day Four!

Today we measure and mark time with birthdays, marriages, events, and such. And when you think about it, the only bad thing about time is that, after Adam's sinful fall, time ultimately brings death. But in heaven, there is no death, so time will be on our side.

Uh, how about restrooms?

So it's a fact that time will be present in heaven. But what about restrooms?

It's always intrigued me that Jesus ate with His disciples after He was raised from the dead and in His resurrected body. Obviously He ate to show He was not a spirit, but rather that He was truly resurrected with flesh and bone.

But that begs the question, Did Jesus go to the restroom during His 40 days on earth, post-resurrection?

> *"See My hands and My feet, that it is I Myself; touch Me and see, for a spirit does not have flesh and bones as you see that I have." And when He had said this, He showed them His hands and His feet. While they still could not believe it because of their joy and amazement, He said to them, "Have you anything here to eat?"* **They gave Him a piece of a broiled fish; and He took it and ate it before them.** *Luke 24:39-43*

Jesus proved to His disciples that His resurrected body had flesh and bone by eating fish. Apparently His resurrected body functioned similarly to His original body.

We also know that when we get to heaven we'll go to the big dinner, called the Marriage Supper of the Lamb (Revelation 19:9). There we'll eat food and drink wine. Jesus said:

> *And He said to them, "I have earnestly desired to eat this Passover with you before I suffer; for I say to you, **I shall never again eat it until it is fulfilled in the kingdom of God.'** And when He had taken a cup and given thanks, He said, 'Take this and share it among yourselves; for I say to you, **I will not drink of the fruit of the vine from now on until the kingdom of God comes."** Lk. 22:15–18*

I've always wondered what the wine was like that Jesus made at the wedding in Cana. So I'm looking forward to tasting His wine at the Marriage Supper! Now it won't be polite to laugh at your Baptist friends who've got no clue what to do. Just saying...

That begs the question

But eating all this food and drinking wine raises another somewhat awkward but interesting question—Will we need to go to the restroom? And if we do go to the restroom, will there only be one for everyone, since in heaven there may be only one sex?

> *For in the resurrection they neither marry nor are given in marriage, but are like angels in heaven. Matt. 22:30*

Then the next obvious question, will there be potties or urinals, or both? Hard to imagine men and women standing side-by-side somehow using a stand-up urinal!

Susie, my wonderful God-given wife of 45 years, came to my rescue on this one. We met at Auburn University where her minor was in physics. She said she believes that our bodies will be so perfect, and the food and wine so perfect, that anything we consume will be perfectly absorbed and nothing will need to be eliminated. Whew! I'm going with that.

> *Our new bodies will be absent of sin and decay.*

Susie makes a good point because we know our new bodies will be like Jesus' resurrected body—flesh and bone—and absent of sin and decay.

> *For our citizenship is in heaven, from which also we eagerly wait for a Savior, the Lord Jesus Christ; **who will transform the body of our humble state into conformity with the body of His glory**, by the exertion of the power that He has even to subject all things to Himself. Phil. 3:20–21*

> *Beloved, now we are children of God, and it has not appeared as yet what we will be. We know that when He appears, **we will be like Him**, because we will see Him just as He is. 1Jn. 3:2*

So when the Rapture whisks us into the sky, we'll leave our wretched sinful bodies behind and they'll be transformed into new eternal containers to house our individual spirits.

> *For we know that if the earthly tent which is our house is torn down, we have a building from God, a **house** not made with hands, **eternal** in the heavens. For indeed in this house we groan, longing to be clothed with our **dwelling from heaven**, inasmuch as we, having put it on, will not be found naked. 2 Cor. 5:1-3*

Our earthly bodies are referred to as temporary tents and our new bodies are referred to as eternal houses. These new bodies won't age or get sick but can walk through walls (John 20:19). That'll be fun!

And no restrooms needed!

CHAPTER NINE

WHEN THE 300-FOOT WAVES SWAMP AMERICA

Yet once more I will shake not only the Earth, but also the heaven. Heb. 12:26

O ne of the most incredible prophecies ever described in the Bible is the magnitude of the mass destruction on the earth during the future Seven-Year Tribulation.

In 1450 BC, back during Israel's Egyptian bondage, God reached a point where He was no longer willing to be silent. He had heard the cries of His people and took amazing action for the world to see and remember...and for the purpose of making His name known.

Then the Egyptians will know that I am the LORD... Ex. 14:18

And today, pretty much the whole world knows about those 10 horrific plagues that God unleashed on Egypt.

When it was all over, there was no doubt in any Egyptian's mind that God was not only God but also that He loved Israel and was actively protecting her.

Fast-forward 3500 years to today and the situation is not much different. God has been quiet for some 2000 years. Miracles have happened, and He has, of course, answered prayers. But nothing has happened that the world could point to like the parting of the Red Sea or making the sun stand still in the sky.

> *...there's a time in the not-too-distant future when the Lord will no longer be silent.*

Yet there's a time in the not-too-distant future when the Lord will no longer be silent. And He will make the 10 plagues look like child's play. When this happens, God will finally deal with all the lying and Biblical sin on the earth. He will protect His name and the world will know He'll be actively protecting Israel.

> *I will magnify Myself, sanctify Myself, and make Myself known in the sight of many nations; and **they will know that I am the LORD**. Ezek. 38:23*

And it's during this blazing wrath unleashed from heaven to earth during the future Seven-year Tribulation that the Bible says God "shakes" not only the earth but also the heavens.

> *There will be signs in sun and moon and stars, and on the earth **dismay among nations**, in perplexity **at the***

roaring of the sea and the waves, men fainting from fear and the expectation of the things which are coming upon the world; for the powers of the heavens will be shaken. Lk. 21:25-26

The Bible says the nations of the world will be in dismay—perplexed by the waves in the seas around the world. Men are falling down, fainting, due to God shaking the heavens and earth so violently.

Therefore I will make the heavens tremble, and the earth will be shaken from its place at the fury of the LORD of hosts in the day of His burning anger. Isa. 13:13

For thus says the LORD of hosts, "Once more [in the future], I am going to shake the heavens and the earth, the sea also and the dry land." Hag. 2:6

Even though it's hard to imagine, the earth is shaken so violently that every island on the planet sinks into the ocean and every mountain is thrown to the ground!

> *...the earth is shaken so violently that every island on the planet sinks...*

That would flatten every building on the planet. From skyscrapers to one-story huts, everything falls flat. That's a lot of shaking going on! Those that survive won't know what to do!

...and they said to the mountains and to the rocks, "Fall on us and hide us from the presence of Him who sits on the throne, and from the wrath of the Lamb..."Rev. 6:16

This will be the post-Rapture moment when He will no longer be silent...

This is the time that the Lord finally says He has had enough of the proud earth-dwellers' sinful lying. This will be the post-Rapture moment when He will no longer be silent and punishes the earth for its Biblical sins like abortion, homosexuality, lying, etc.

No one is getting away with anything; it will all eventually come to light.

> *For the LORD of hosts will have a day of reckoning against everyone who is proud and lofty and against everyone who is lifted up, that he may be abased.... against all the lofty mountains, against all the hills that are lifted up... Isa. 2:12,14*

And in His righteous anger that's been quiet for 2000 years, He shakes the earth quite violently.

> *The fish of the sea, the birds of the heavens, the beasts of the field, all the creeping things that creep on the earth, and all the men who are on the face of the earth will shake at My presence; **the mountains also will***

be thrown down, the steep pathways will collapse and every wall will fall to the ground. Ezek 38:20

And every island fled away, and the mountains were not found. Rev. 16:20

Now when the earth is shaken so violently that the mountains all over the earth are thrown down and the islands sink in the oceans, enormous waves will be created. And they'll come crashing to shores worldwide.

We're talking 300- to 500-foot waves submerging New York, Los Angeles, Miami, New Orleans, and Seattle. All coastal cities in the USA and around the world will be devastated for miles inland.

I wrote in Chapter 7 of *Steel on Steel Book 1* about the probability that the latter-day Babylon prophecies of future destruction could easily be a parallel reference to the United States. I detailed 23 verses in the Bible that latter-day "Babylon" could be referring only to the United States.

The sea has come up over Babylon; She has been engulfed with its tumultuous waves. Jer. 51:42

If I'm correct, then these references about this end-time city being engulfed by water would be a prophecy for New York City's total destruction.

For the LORD is going to destroy Babylon, and He will make her loud noise vanish from her. And their waves will roar like many waters... Jer. 51:55

This is the exultant city which dwells securely, who says in her heart, "I am, and there is no one besides me." How she has become a desolation, a resting place for beasts!... Zeph. 2:15

New York will still be leveled during the Tribulation destruction...

However, even if I'm wrong about New York City being the future Babylon that is destroyed, New York will still be leveled during the Tribulation destruction caused from the worldwide violent earthquakes and gigantic waves created when God shakes the earth. It's such a destructive time that Mark says this:

Unless the Lord had shortened those days, no life would have been saved; but for the sake of the elect, whom He chose, He shortened the days. Mk. 13:20

We as Believers won't be on the earth. Thankfully, God promises we're not recipients of His wrath. God will Rapture us away before His wrath comes to Earth.

*For God has **not destined us for wrath**, but for obtaining salvation through our Lord Jesus Christ... 1Thes. 5:9*

We're 100% sure that all that unimaginable destruction is coming because God said

Prophecy is so important that some 30% of the entire Bible is prophetic...

it would. You can bank on it because all past prophecies were fulfilled literally and the Lord is consistent.

Behold, the former things have come to pass, now I declare new things; Before they spring forth I proclaim them to you. Isa. 42:9

God gave us Bible prophecy to PROVE He is God. Only God can predict specifics in the future with exact precision recorded in Scripture. He has recorded prophecies in the past as a testament to being God. Prophecy is so important that some 30% of the entire Bible is prophetic in nature.

Dead Ahead

The Bible gives us a sobering admonition directed to those of us living in the Church Age...

And His voice shook the earth then, but now He has promised, saying, "YET ONCE MORE I WILL SHAKE

NOT ONLY THE EARTH, BUT ALSO THE HEAVEN."
This expression, "Yet once more," denotes the removing
of those things which can be shaken, as of created things,
so that those things which cannot be shaken may
remain. Therefore, since we receive a kingdom which
cannot be shaken, let us show gratitude, by which we
may offer to God an acceptable service with reverence
and awe; for our God is a consuming fire. Heb. 12:26-29

The world may laugh and sneer at God today, but we
know in the not-too-distant future our God will remove
His Church and then He will come out of His quietness like
a consuming fire. And it will be a never-ending nightmare
for those left behind.

In the meantime, we'll continue to honor our Creator
God with gratitude and reverence while looking for oppor-
tunities to share what Jesus has done in our lives.

Use us, Lord, to be a light to a dark, unsuspecting world!

CHAPTER TEN

SHOULD CHRISTIANS CELEBRATE "EASTER"?

It's not the word "Easter" that's the problem...

Over the last 50 years or so, many people have written about the pagan origins of the word "Easter." And, despite the word being used in the KJV translation in Acts 12:4, a lot of Believers in good Bible-teaching churches have been taught that "Easter" can be linked to the fertility Goddess Astarte and other such proclamations.

I, too, had read several reference books that bemoaned Easter as a "Satanic" holiday. Hearing all the (mis)information caused me to offer rewards to my children if they could go the entire Resurrection Day holiday without saying the word "Easter."

But in 2016, Roger Patterson of Answers In Genesis wrote an excellently researched article showing the misinformation and myths floating around that supposedly tie "Easter" to a number of Satanic origins.[1]

> **"Easter"**
> is a translation/
> transliteration of the
> word "resurrection"
> and it's roots can be
> traced to solid Believers
> during the Reformation.

Patterson convincingly showed that the word "Easter" was a translation / transliteration of the word "resurrection" and its roots could be traced to solid Believers during the Reformation. He pointed out that the basis for which the connection between Easter and Astarte is made is like saying, "Since Babylon was called the 'Golden City,' then McDonald's 'golden arches' must be rooted in Satanic ritual." And, of course, that dog just won't hunt!

And now the myths of Easter's origins have been repeated so long and so often that most believe them to be fact... when they're not facts at all. I've made apologies to my children.

Just to be clear, Easter bunnies and colored eggs ARE terrible—in a league with Santa Claus, the horrible Jesus substitute. See "Santa's Claws, Satan's Claws" in *Steel on Steel Book 2*.[2]

But the word "Easter" actually comes from the German root word for "Resurrection." And the reformers of Martin Luther's day were the first to use the word, which had zero connection to Astarte the fertility god. So much for making "Easter" the bad guy.

That being said, I still believe we should call the day of Jesus' resurrection "Resurrection Sunday," if for no other reason than to make the point that it has nothing to do with the Easter bunny and colored eggs.

The Real Problem

However, there IS a real BIG PROBLEM with the DATE we celebrate Resurrection Sunday—of which few Christians seem to be aware. And even though almost all Protestant churches will continue to celebrate Easter or Resurrection Sunday on the verifiably wrong Sunday, it's important for Believers to know when and why it should be celebrated.

Currently, there are four big days that Church Age Believers could make a case to celebrate each year: 1) The Birth of Jesus. 2) The Death of Jesus. 3) The Resurrection of Jesus. 4) The Arrival of God's Holy Spirit to indwell Believers on earth.

Two of the four get a lot of attention from Believers: Christmas and Resurrection Day.

There IS a real BIG PROBLEM with the DATE we celebrate Resurrection Sunday.

The Day Jesus Was Born

The Bible doesn't give us a clue when Jesus was born. He was unlikely to have been born on December 25, but hey, maybe He was conceived on that date and born in September.

Since the Lord didn't reveal the date, there's no problem celebrating His birth on December 25. Thankfully the whole world celebrates His birth together, even though Satan has pretty much hijacked Christmas with presents, parties, and Santa—anything to keep the public away from the real meaning of Christmas.

The Day Jesus Died

Jesus died during the Passover celebration, likely in 33 AD. Nissan 14 fell on Friday that year. Jesus was nailed to the cross the day before on Nissan 13, the Day of Preparation at the same time the thousands of other sheep and goats were being slaughtered as Passover blood sacrifices. The Passover meal was eaten that evening, Nissan 14, which began at 6 pm (instead of midnight).

> *Jesus was nailed to the cross the day before on Nissan 13, the Day of Preparation.*

The Day Jesus Was Resurrected

But the Lord DID tell us when the Resurrection occurred—on the Feast of First Fruits, which is celebrated the day after the Shabbat (Saturday) that follows Nissan 14 day of Passover (Friday in 33 AD), which was Sunday.

Therefore, the Resurrection occurred the Sunday after the Passover Shabbat, on the Feast of First Fruits, and we should be celebrating Resurrection Sunday on the first Sunday following the Jewish Passover. They are tied together by Scripture. The Jews go to great lengths to celebrate the Passover meal on the correct date that God instructed, on Nissan 14.

They observed the Passover in the first month [Nissan], on the fourteenth day of the month, at twilight, in the wilderness of Sinai; according to all that the LORD had commanded Moses... Num. 9:5

So it's not rocket science to know what day the Jewish Passover meal should be celebrated—it's Nissan 14 on the Hebrew calendar—and all we have to do is celebrate Jesus' Resurrection Day on Feast of First Fruits, which is the Sunday following Passover. **But often we don't!**

Strangely, the date we celebrate Easter/Resurrection Sunday has no connection to Passover, and sometimes it doesn't even fall on Passover week! In 2015 we missed the correct Resurrection Day by a month!

It's important to note that Nissan 14 is not a fixed day of the week and therefore the Jewish Passover celebration date moves around each year. 2016 Passover/Nissan 14 fell on April 21. The correct Resurrection Day should have been April 24. But the Catholic Easter Date had us incorrectly celebrating it on March 27!

> *...it's not rocket science to know what day the Jewish Passover meal should be celebrated...*

In 2020, Passover/Nissan 14 fell on Wednesday, April 8, and we correctly celebrated Resurrection Day on the following Sunday, April 12. But in 2024, Passover/Nissan 14 is April 22, and Resurrection Day should be April 28. But the Catholic Easter date has us celebrating Resurrection on March 31, over a month off!

Why are the Dates Off?

So what happened that made Christians start celebrating Easter/Resurrection Sunday on the wrong dates every few years? The answer is rooted in Catholic anti-Semitism.

...in 325 AD, the first Council of Nicaea met. These were Catholic Bishops...

By the early fourth century, most church leaders were still celebrating Passover on Nisan 14 as Jesus' crucifixion day and Resurrection Day on the following Sunday. But in 325 AD, the first Council of Nicaea met. These were Catholic Bishops gathered by Constantine in the city of Nicaea.

This group of Church leaders addressed and voted on several theological issues, including the issue of what day to celebrate Resurrection Day—the 14th of Nissan (Passover) or the Sunday following the 14th.

The Nicaean Bishops dismissed Nissan 14 having anything to do with Easter because they wanted to distance themselves from the Jewish Passover. The Catholics believed that because the Jews killed Jesus the Church had inherited all the Biblical blessings from God; therefore, the Jews were forever out of God's favor.

This anti-Semitic view of God's chosen people still prevails today in the Catholic Church. But it gets worse! Not wanting to connect anything to the Jewish Passover, they also discarded the Sunday following Passover, the Feast of First Fruits, as the day to celebrate Easter. These Catholic Bishops simply decided against using Scripture to determine the date.

Instead, they decided that Easter/Resurrection Day should be completely unrelated to a Scripturally based Passover date! Good grief, what were they smoking?

The Bishops instead came up with their own ridiculous and unbiblical way to determine when Resurrection Day should be celebrated! Specifically, they decided Easter should fall on "the first Sunday following the first ecclesiastical full-moon that occurs on or after the day of the vernal equinox." The vernal equinox is when the sun crosses the equator in the spring, which is the first day of spring.

By the Catholic Church basing the Resurrection Sunday date on the moon and the first day of spring, it removed any possibility of Easter being connected to Passover!

Not wanting to connect anything to the Jewish Passover, they ... discarded the Sunday following Passover...

And it bases the date on the sun, moon, and stars, for heaven's sake.

*And beware not to lift up your eyes to heaven and see
the sun and the moon and the stars, all the host of heaven, and be drawn away and worship them and serve
them, those which the LORD your God has allotted to
all the peoples under the whole heaven. Deut. 4:19*

They explain this blasphemous way to determine the
Easter date this way on catholic.com, answering the question "How is Easter Sunday determined?"

After first admitting that Easter SHOULD immediately
follow Passover, which occurs on Nissan 14, they then add:

> ***They decided
> Easter would be
> celebrated on
> the first Sunday
> after the full
> Paschal moon.***

"Christians didn't like being dependent on the pronouncements of
rabbis for how to celebrate Christian feasts so they (the Council
of Nicaea) came up with another
way of determining the date. They
decided that Easter would be
celebrated on the first Sunday after
(never on) the Paschal full moon."[3]

Really? Let's think about that for a moment... God, not
man, established the specific day for Passover to be celebrated, Nissan 14. This was one of the greatest days in the
entire Old Testament. Jews were commanded to celebrate
the day each year with a feast, forever! And Jesus rose from
the dead the following Sunday.

And since Believers are adopted/grafted into the Jewish promises, we technically have Jewish spiritual roots!

*...**adoption** as sons through Jesus Christ... Eph. 1:5*

*...**grafted** in... Rom. 11:17*

We should embrace our Jewish heritage, not discard it! But the Catholic Church was so corrupt and so anti-Semitic it severed Passover from being connected to Jesus, even though the Bible says the Resurrection is forever tied to Passover and the Jewish feasts.

> *...the spiritually defiant leaders of the Catholic Church decided to change the date of the Resurrection...*

Rather than connect Resurrection Day to the Passover and celebrate our Jewish roots, the spiritually defiant leaders of the Catholic Church decided to change the date of the Resurrection so as not to be connected to the Jewish Passover!

That is like changing/adding to God's Word—which is NOT GOOD!

*I testify to everyone who hears the words of the prophecy of this book: **if anyone adds to them**, God will add to him the plagues which are written in this book... Rev. 22:18*

This was Satan at his best—getting the Catholic Church to wrongly loathe Israel and the Jews so much they didn't want to be associated in any way with the Jewish Passover.

All this stems from the Catholics holding to a pitifully inaccurate Amillennial doctrinal stance ... foolishly believing the Church has inherited God's promises to the Jews. This also proves the incredible importance of accurately understanding Bible prophecy!

If you have the wrong eschatological position, it will distort how you interpret the Scriptures.

Correct Eschatology Chart:

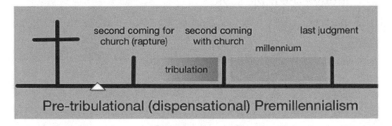

Incorrect Eschatology Chart (Catholic):

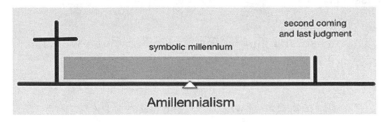

The Catholic Church holds to an Amillennial position, which means they don't take Scripture literally.

For instance, they take the six references to a "thousand years" of Jesus' reign on earth to mean a "long time." Correctly using a literal translation, we understand that Jesus will reign 1000 years on the earth as King. If the Catholic Church properly viewed the Scriptures literally, they would be Premillennial and embrace the Jews as God's chosen people.

But their poor doctrine and anti-Semitic views blinded them to the point that they incorrectly changed the day we celebrate Resurrection Day. And later, the breakaway Protestants kept the Catholic Easter dates.

But we can't be too hard on the Catholics. Martin Luther also misunderstood and loathed Israel and the Jewish people.[4] Although he was correct with his protesting of Catholic Church doctrines and policies, God did not reveal to him at that time the Catholic Church's incorrect eschatology positions.

> *But we can't be too hard on the Catholics...*

In fact, Catholic eschatological error continued to be passed down to Protestant denominations for another 100 years or so before Premillennial defenses finally exposed the error of Amillennial theology.

Summary

So to nail shut the case for which day we should be celebrating Resurrection Day, we need to quit being led by the incorrect calendar dates of the Catholic Church. Instead, we should use the Scripturally commanded Nissan 14 date to determine which Sunday to celebrate.

Bottom line, Resurrection Day should be the Sunday following Passover. The "official" Easter is not tied to Passover—and it should be!

So if you're a pastor reading this, do you have the spiritual conviction to celebrate Resurrection Day on the Sunday following the Jewish Passover in the years to come? Or are you just going to continue using the incorrect dating of the Catholic Church? Pray about it!

References
1) https://answersingenesis.org/holidays/easter/is-the-name-easter-of-pagan-origin/
2) Satan's Claws/Santa's Claws; Steal on Steal, Book 2, Chapter 5
3) https://www.catholic.com/qa/how-is-easter-sunday-determined-palm-sunday-ash-wednesday
4) http://www.jewishvirtuallibrary.org/martin-luther-quot-the-jews-and-their-lies-quot

CHAPTER ELEVEN

LIGHT FROM DISTANT STARS— MILLIONS OF YEARS?

He stretches out the north over empty space and hangs the earth on nothing. Job 26:7

When you look up at a starry sky at night, you are actually viewing some of the trillions times trillions of suns in the universe.[1] All but a few of what we are seeing are the lights from distant suns.

Each of these suns is like our sun, although our sun is one of the smaller ones. And each sun has a solar system around it like ours.

So our universe is one behemoth area. It's so large, in fact, how in the world do you defend a literal translation of the Bible's six-day creation 6000 years ago when it takes light millions of years to get here from distant planets?

There are two good answers, both of which help explain how millions of years of light shine from the stars at night.

1. **God created Adam and Eve full grown.** They were
    created with the appearance of age. He did the same
    with the trees and animals. So he certainly could
    have created the universe with the appearance of age.

2. **God "stretched out" the heavens.** There are Scrip-
    tures that discuss the creation and address the heav-
    ens being formed. The prophet Isaiah mentioned
    three times that God created the heavens and then
    stretched them out:

*Thus says God the LORD, who created the heavens and
stretched them out... Isa. 42:5*

*It is I who made the earth, and created man upon it. I
stretched out the heavens with My hands, and I ordained all their host. Isa. 45:12*

*That you have forgotten the LORD your Maker, Who
stretched out the heavens, and laid the foundations of
the earth... Isa. 51:13*

This indicates that
God created all the
stars closer around
the earth and then
stretched them out
to the far ends of the
universe... their light
stretching with them.

God spoke the universe into existence!

By the word of the LORD the heavens were made, and by the breath of His mouth all their host. Psa. 33:6

For He spoke, and it was done; He commanded, and it stood fast. Psa. 33:9

If the Lord spoke the universe into being, He could do anything He wished to do. And He can't lie, so what the Bible says is true.

Bottom line, if the Lord can speak the heavens into existence in a moment, He can easily create the light from the stars at the same time. Nothing is too difficult for God.

> *God spoke the universe into existence!*

Behold, I am the LORD, the God of all flesh; is anything too difficult for Me? Jer. 32:27

Reference

1) The number of suns in the universe is estimated to be 1 with 24 zeros following!

CHAPTER TWELVE

TYING TASSELS TO TRUTH

*Above: In Hebrew "Yahweh" is read from right to left.
You're going to love what the letters spell out!*

Believers in the United States today pretty much take for granted living their lives with access to their Bible to study and learn God's Word. But for most of the world's history, that was not the case!

Since the invention of the printing press in the 15th century, the Word of God can be read regularly—not only by church leaders but also by regular common folk.

But for the first 3000 years of God's recorded Word, access to God's inspired Word came only from hearing pieces of it read on Shabbat. Rarely did Levites, much less

non-Levites, have a personally owned scroll to read in their spare time.

Back in the Old Testament days, God's inspired Word that was given to Moses and the prophets was painstakingly copied and recopied on animal skins. It took a whole year for one person to copy the first five books, Genesis to Deuteronomy, called the Pentateuch.

So usually the only way you could learn Scripture was attending Saturday Shabbat, when the Jewish leaders would read a predetermined portion of the Pentateuch, mandatorily completing the entire Pentateuch in one year before beginning it over again.

Other Scriptures from books like Daniel, Psalms, or Ruth were also read to supplement that week's teaching.

To remember what **to do** and **to not do** from what you heard on Shabbat was an obvious problem. There are 613 laws in those first five books—248 are "to do" and 365 are "to not do." That's a lot to learn if you're only hearing them in pieces on Saturdays!

Therefore, in the 15th chapter of the Book of Numbers, the Lord dealt with this tremendous responsibility. It begins with the Lord laying down several requirements about keeping the Law and the penalty of death if someone defiantly breaks the Law. But the Lord also made a provision for dealing with people who unintentionally break the Law without realizing they did.

Moses then records the story of a man who was caught gathering wood/working on the Sabbath. Exodus 31:14-15 clearly states no work shall be done on Shabbat and the penalty was death if you did.

The Lord told the congregation, through Moses, to stone the man to death for breaking the Law, which they did. He apparently had willfully broken the Law—he knew it was wrong—so no exception could be made for not realizing what he had done.

> *To Believers today, this seems harsh. But Israel lived and died under the exactness of God's Law.*

To Believers today, this seems harsh. But Israel lived and died under the exactness of God's Law. Remember what happened to Uzzah's good intentions when he steadied the Ark and God struck him dead! (2Samuel 6:3-8)

However, the very next thing recorded in Scripture says if someone unintentionally broke the Law, a sacrifice was offered to the Lord and he was forgiven. It is specific in Numbers 15:22-26 and summarized a couple of verses later:

> *You shall have one law for him who does anything **unintentionally**, for him who is native among the sons of*

Israel and for the alien who sojourns among them. But the person who does anything defiantly, whether he is native or an alien, that one is blaspheming the LORD; and that person shall be cut off from among his people. Num. 15:29-30

So as Jews learned the Law on Shabbat in their synagogues, they were held responsible for their future actions if they knowingly broke the Law—many of which had a death penalty associated with breaking it.

To help keep the Israelites from forgetting that they were under the Law and to remind them of the penalty for breaking the Law, God commanded them to hang blue tassels on their garments. This is usually done today by hanging blue tassels on the corners of their robes and/or prayer shawls.

*The LORD also spoke to Moses, saying, "Speak to the sons of Israel, and tell them that they shall **make for themselves tassels on the corners of their garments** throughout their generations, and that they shall put on the tassel of each corner a cord of blue. It shall be a tassel for you to look **at and remember all the commandments** of the LORD, so as to do them and not follow after your own heart and your own eyes, after*

which you played the harlot, so that you may remember
to do all My commandments and be holy to your God."
Num. 15:37-40

Today, when a Jew wears his tassels (often referred to
as tzitzits) on the four corners of his prayer shawl, he ties
them in such a way that the knots spell out "Yahweh," the
name of God.

They can do this because in Hebrew each letter represents a number. Yahweh is actually spelled in four Hebrew letters: *yod, hey, veh, hey.* The corresponding numbers
are:

- yod = 10
- hey = 5
- veh = 6
- hey = 5

So **most** of the Jews would create their tassels by wrap-
ping the blue cord in a line in groups of 10, 5, 6, 5, with
each group separated by two white knots. Therefore, when
they looked at the tassels, they saw spelled out "yod hey
vey hey" or "Yahweh."

Naturally, not all Jews agree. Some Jews disagree with
the 10-5-6-5 numbers and rather tie their knots in a 7-8-11-
13 sequence. But the point is, they all tie their tassel knots
in a way that reminds them to obey Yahweh.

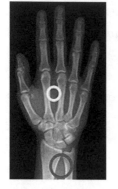

What's really fascinating is what the Hebrew letters in the name Yahweh actually mean.

Yod means "**hand**," specifically from the wrist to the tips of the fingers.

[Note: There is a different letter, *kaf,* that means palm. This is important because **Jesus was nailed through His wrists (gray circle)**. If you nail someone to a cross with nails in the palms (white circle), the weight of the body will tear the soft skin and the person will fall off the cross! There is more on Roman crucifixion in Chapter 15.]

Hey means to "**behold**," "show," or "reveal."

Vey signifies a **nail**, peg, or hook. It even looks like a nail.

So when you read Yahweh from right to left in the Hebrew, it reads:

"Behold the nail, behold the hand." Or simply, "Behold the nailed hand."

When you combine the meaning for the individual letters with the overall meaning of the word Yahweh, YHWH, which means "salvation," then it translates to:

"Behold, the nailed hand is salvation."

So today, the Jews who so meticulously and piously tie their tassels so they can read the name Yahweh are looking directly at their true salvation—Jesus' blood from the nailed wrists as the propitiation for their sins.

When God said He would blind the Jews, He meant what He said! Only a few Jews become Believers in the Church Age. And most of those who do get saved struggle with legalism, struggle with getting away from the Law. They tend to want to work Jesus into the Law instead of making Jesus' and Paul's instructions their life's focus.

Getting back to God's instructions to the Israelites to tie those tassels to remember His Commandments, we can certainly apply it to us living in the Church Age.

What is it that we need to do to remember God's Word on a moment-by-moment basis?

From the Old Testament we have:

Your word I have treasured in my heart, that I may not sin against You. Psa. 119:11

From the New Testament we have:

Therefore, take up the full armor of God... His Word.
Eph. 6:13

To armor up, we're to know the Word of God. Now, more than ever, we need to know God's Word to discern good and evil. Satan is a liar, and the Word sheds light to discern truth from lies.

CHAPTER THIRTEEN

AMERICA'S HEAD DEMON
And how he's hammering us to the far left...

Let's begin with a short review of angels.... All angels were created good until Satan, one of the top three angels, sinned.

> *You were blameless in your ways from the day you were created until unrighteousness was found in you.*
> *Ezek. 28:15*

Satan is quite clever. He's had some 6,000 years of practice lying to humans about who he is and what he's up to. Too many Christians think of him as a red-tailed, red-faced demonic-looking character. And the Bible says the world is going to be shocked to actually see him when he is cast to earth in the middle of the Tribulation.

> *And the great dragon was thrown down, the serpent of old who is called the devil and Satan, **who deceives the***

whole world; he was thrown down to the earth, and his angels were thrown down with him. Rev. 12:9

*Those who see you will gaze at you, they will ponder over you, saying, **"Is this the man who made the earth tremble, who shook kingdoms..."** Isa. 14:16*

...born-again Believers will continue to live as outcasts on Satan's earth.

So it is more likely for Satan to actually end up looking and sounding like a cross between Megyn Kelly and Tom Cruise than a gross and evil-looking guy.

The point is that Satan is actually quite beautiful and wise...because he was created perfect!

*...Thus says the Lord GOD, 'You had the seal of **perfection,** full of **wisdom** and perfect in **beauty.**' Ezek. 28:12*

*Your heart was lifted up because of your **beauty;** You corrupted your **wisdom** by reason of your **splendor.** Ezek. 28:17*

But until the day the Lord takes His believers away at the Rapture, we'll continue to live as outcasts on Satan's earth. Never forget that Satan, the devil, took control of this world illegally through deception in the Garden of Eden. He lied!

*...there is no truth in him. Whenever he speaks a lie, he speaks from his own nature, for **he is a liar** and the **father of lies**. Jn. 8:44*

He began in a lie and continues to lie. And he wrongly rules the earth today. The Bible actually calls Satan the "...god of this world..."

*...in whose case **the god of this world** has blinded the minds of the unbelieving so they might not see the light of the gospel of the glory of Christ, who is the image of God. 2Cor. 4:4*

Satan loathes us Believers and continually points at our sins (Revelation 12:10). He wants us to have a poor and pitiful testimony.

*Be of sober spirit, be on the alert. Your adversary, the devil, prowls about like a roaring lion, **seeking someone to devour**. 1Pet. 5:8*

Fortunately, greater is God Who is in us than Satan who is in the world (1John 4:4).

So we're aliens on this planet, thankfully trusting God to protect us while we wait for Jesus to return and take His rightful place on the throne on Mt. Moriah in Jerusalem. This earth will be wonderfully different with Jesus on the throne as the rightful God of this world!

Satan's fall from grace

In the Garden of Eden when Satan fell, he took one third of all God's angels with him in revolt. We call these fallen angels demons. The good news is that there are two good angels for every one fallen angel!

Demons are angels

Demons are simply fallen angels who were created by God to serve Him, but they followed Satan instead. Demons are cruel and unjust and want Believers to keep their eyes off eternal things that count and on worldly concerns that don't.

> *In the meantime, Satan still has millions of demons at his disposal.*

The really, Really, REALLY bad angels were locked up after Noah's flood in the center of the earth—in a place called the "bottomless pit." These were the ones who mated with humans, making a real mess here on earth...and God had to destroy the earth and start over with Noah's family (Genesis 6).

These pre-flood demons will be released in the Tribulation to once again wreak havoc on the world (Revelation 9:2). One can only imagine how bad that will be.

In the meantime, Satan still has millions of demons at his disposal. Not surprisingly, he has assigned the worst of his evil ones as head demons over every country in the world.

The Bible talks about the head demon of Greece and the head demon of Persia—the area we now call Iran. Michael the archangel fought against these head-of-country demons:

> *But the prince of the kingdom of **Persia** was withstanding me for twenty-one days; then behold, Michael, one of the chief princes, came to help me, for I had been left there with the kings of Persia.* Dan. 10:13

> *Then he said, "Do you under-stand why I came to you? But I shall now return to fight against the prince of **Persia**; so I am going forth, and behold, the prince of **Greece** is about to come." Dan. 10:20*

These demons do Satan's bidding to disrupt, crush, and weaken as many humans and nations as possible, 24/7.

These demons do Satan's bidding to disrupt, crush, and weaken as many humans and nations as possible, 24/7.

> *How you have fallen from heaven, O star of the morning, son of the dawn! You have been cut down to the earth, **you who have weakened the nations!**" Isa. 14:12*

Therefore, if Satan has assigned a demon over each country, then we know America has a head demon. And America's head demon (hereafter referred to as AHD) has obviously been quite active, opposing all of God's truth at every turn and substituting and promoting Satan's godless vile agenda. AHD's job is to tear down anything godly and promote anything ungodly. But he is being restrained more than most head demons due to the vast number of born-again Believers who house the Restrainer—the restraining power of God's Holy Spirit.

> *AHD has been making MAJOR strides in the last 50 years...*

I'm guessing that when Satan holds his meetings for his top demons to report successes and failures, for the last 250 years or so, AHD has been the low demon on the totem pole.

I'm sure it's been a struggle for him having to deal with the prayers from all the Believers in the U.S. I'm quite certain that in those meetings Satan has snarled and been livid with AHD for not getting any decent traction for wholesale evil. Until recently anyway.

AHD has been making MAJOR strides in the last 50 years. AHD has made inroads into deceiving many of our American leaders using a not-so-obvious behind-the-scenes plan. Fifty years ago he didn't openly come out pro-homosexual, pro-abortion, or pro-evolution. He didn't openly rail against business, Christians, Israel, and America's strong churches.

Rather, AHD went about his tasks slowly, almost unnoticed. Tirelessly working night and day (demons don't sleep), he weakened the foundations that made America great.

AHD was poised for the big coup mainly through making money more important to Americans than God. And when money is your God, economic entrapment always follows.

Almost half of America is on the receiving end of government subsidies in one form or another. Federal and state taxes are out of control, taking some 50% of all income. That rascal had the bit in his mouth and was ready to run!

But by the grace of God, a new sheriff came to town and began cleaning up a bit. Not sure how long it will last, but grateful nonetheless.

> *...he weakened the foundations that made America great.*

Pray for President Trump and for our country's leadership. When our leadership changes again, and it will, the takeover could be swift and destructive.

Use this temporary reprieve wisely!

CHAPTER FOURTEEN

SHOULD CHRISTIANS FAST?

*But you, when you fast, anoint your head and wash
your face so that your fasting will not be noticed by men,
but by your Father who is in secret; and your Father
who sees what is done in secret will reward you.*
Matt. 6:17-18

As explained in Chapter 2, here is another example of needing to view scripture through a dispensational framework.

Several years ago I was discussing with an elder the pros and cons of a huge decision our church was facing. He ended our conversation saying, "But we've got it all under control because all the elders are fasting." I looked at him incredulously and said, "Really? You think that will help?" The conversation went downhill from there.

Fasting didn't help these men make a better decision or make them better attuned to the Lord's direction. The decision they made was disastrous, but it had nothing to do with them fasting or not fasting. These well-meaning and otherwise Godly men were simply incorrectly applying statements in the Gospels, things Jesus said to the Jews under the Law, to people living post-cross in the Church Age.

> *But the truth is, there is zero you can do or not do to make yourself more or less acceptable to God.*

Applying this elder's reasoning, it's easy to see why so many people through the years have punished their bodies trying to get God's attention.

On our trips to the Holyland, we've often seen people bleeding from beating their backs with whips or crawling on their bloodied knees for blocks, believing that these kinds of actions would make God more likely to answer their prayers.

But the truth is, there is zero you, as a believer, can do or not do to make yourself more or less acceptable to God. You can't, but Jesus could, and He paid (past tense) the price with His Blood shed on the cross.

> *...(Jesus) said, "It is finished!" And He bowed His head and gave up His spirit. Jn. 19:30*

The phrase "It is finished" is a Greek accounting term meaning "paid in full." Born-again Believers are as holy as they'll ever be living in their sinful and temporary container. You can't add to the righteousness Jesus provided you. He doesn't need your help.

Nothing can be added to the cross.

Therefore, Paul, our Church Age Apostle, never mentioned fasting. In fact, he said there is zero you can do to make yourself more pure, or more acceptable to God.

> *You foolish Galatians, who has bewitched you, before whose eyes Jesus Christ was publicly portrayed as crucified? This is the only thing I want to find out from you: did you receive the Spirit by the works of the Law, or by hearing with faith? **Are you so foolish? Having begun by the Spirit, are you now being perfected by the flesh?** Gal. 3:1-3*

With the exception of a couple of references to people fasting in the transitional book of Acts, it's not commanded or instructed by Paul or any other leader in the Church Age.

The phrase "It is finished" is a Greek accounting term meaning "paid in full."

Some people have used this verse to justify Believers fasting:

> *And Jesus said to them, "While the bridegroom is with them, the attendants of the bridegroom cannot fast, can they? So long as they have the bridegroom with them, they cannot fast. But the days will come when the bridegroom is taken away from them, and then they will fast in that day." Mk. 2:19-20*

They suggest that verse confirms that while Jesus is away we should fast. That's true for the Jews who rejected their Messiah, to whom this was written. But this verse actually confirms Church Age believers are NOT to fast because He's not gone away—He lives in us!

Is Fasting Sinful?

> *If you want wisdom, just ask for it.*

Fasting may have some health benefits, and I'm obviously referring only to spiritual applications. So it's not necessarily wrong to fast. It's just wrong to fast thinking it will make God more likely to answer your prayers or impart more wisdom to you.

If you want wisdom, just ask for it.

> *But if any of you lacks wisdom, let him ask of God, **who gives to all generously** and without reproach, and it will be given to him. James 1:5*

CHAPTER FIFTEEN

JESUS' FIVE WOUNDS

Jesus' death was both prophetic and well documented. Isaiah 53 is uncomfortable reading for Jews who try to dismiss Jesus as anything but God's Son.

> *But He was pierced through for our transgressions, He was crushed for our iniquities; The chastening for our well-being fell upon Him, and by His scourging we are healed. Isa. 53:5*

> *...and He Himself bore our sins in His body on the cross, that we might die to sin and live to righteousness; for by His wounds you were healed. 1Pet. 2:24*

Jesus had five "pierced" wounds from His crucifixion: two in His wrists, two in His feet, and one in His side. That's an interesting number because five is God's number for grace.

But our healing is permanent only after our transition from this life to the next—what the secular world calls earthly death.

It's important to note that Christians actually don't die, they just change places. When a Believer dies, he/she is immediately with the Lord.

> ...we are of good courage, I say, and prefer rather to be absent from the body and to be at home with the Lord. 2Cor. 5:8

During the Roman Empire, crucifixion was the worst death sentence you could receive. Often people lived days in agony before dying on a cross.

In some of the recently released Christian-oriented movies, the person being crucified is **incorrectly shown to be nailed through the palm of the hand.**

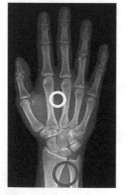

But actually, the Romans never nailed people to a cross by nailing through the palm of their hands.

There is nothing but flesh to hold up the weight of the body on the cross if the nails were driven through the palm of the hands (see white circle to left). If nailed through the palm, the flesh would tear away in the first hour or so.

Therefore, the person was nailed just above the wrist (see gray circle at bottom of previous page) between the two large bones in the forearm, in order to hold the person up on the crossbar indefinitely.

Since the prisoner might hang on the cross for days, the Romans would also nail a piece of wood as sort of a washer to keep the nails from pulling through.

Also, apparently crucified people writhed a lot in their pain and the repetitive back-and-forth motion would sometimes loosen the nails

and pull them out of the wood, offering temporary relief to the person.

So to keep that from happening, the nail was driven through the wood and bent on the back side, securing the hands and feet to the wood.

The feet were turned sideways, pushed up and under the buttocks and nailed together into the wooden post.

This made it difficult to push up with the legs, leaving most of the weight on the arms. This bodily configuration made it most difficult to even take a single breath. To breathe, the prisoner had to both pull up with the arms while pushing up with the legs as best they could manage.

The word in the Greek for "hands" is "*cheir*," which does mean "hands," but can also mean **any part of the lower arm below the elbow.**

An example of using the word *"cheir"* to mean the lower arms is in Acts 12:7 where the text says the chains fell from Peter's "hands." Was Peter chained around his hands? No, obviously he was chained around his wrists.

So it's probable that pictures depicting Jesus straight-legged, with underwear and ropes around his arms to hold Him up, are incorrect.

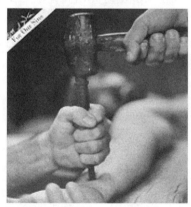

Photo by Jodie Yelton

Unbelievably, He was instead crucified more like the depictions shown in these drawings.

It was horrific torture that the Creator God of the universe willingly endured in order to atone for our sin.

Yes, the spiritual purchase was the most important aspect of Jesus' death, burial, and resurrection. But the physical pain should never be downplayed.

Keep that in mind the next time you celebrate Easter / Resurrection Week.

Reference

Living in the Time of Jesus of Nazareth, by Peter Connolly, Steimatzky Publishers, 1983.

CHAPTER SIXTEEN

SIGNS OF JESUS' RETURN

G od gave us Bible prophecy to prove He is God because no one can predict the future with 100% accuracy except God. Nostradamus had about 5% of his quite-vague prophecies come true. But the Bible has never missed one iota, even predicting names of people hundreds of years in advance.

It's interesting that over 25% of Scripture is regarding short- or long-term prophecies. So it's hard to read much in the Bible that doesn't touch on Bible prophecy.

When we take groups to Israel, we always schedule a Bible study on the top of the Mount of Olives. It is a stunning view looking down Palm Sunday Road, across the Garden of Gethsemane toward the Old City and Temple Mount. There's so much Bible history from that breath-taking vantage point that it's always one of our

longest Bible studies of the entire tour—and also the most interesting!

From there, you can see the locations of the first two Jewish Temples as well as trace the final week of Jesus prior to the cross. You can see from the Empty Tomb area on the right (north) to the Pool of Siloam on the left (south).

But sitting at the top of Mount of Olives also gives us pause to reflect on the story of Jesus riding humbly on the donkey in that very spot. In the middle of that fascinating event, the Bible says **when Jesus saw that same view** of Jerusalem, he wept bitterly.

> *When He approached Jerusalem, He saw the city and wept over it, saying, "If you had known in this day, even you, the things which make for peace! But now they have been hidden from your eyes.... because you did not recognize the time of your visitation."*
> *Lk. 19:41-42, 44*

Jesus did more than weep. In English we would say "He sobbed." Jesus sobbed over the fact that the Jews missed the day that was fulfilled exactly as prophesied by Daniel.

Jesus held the Jews accountable for knowing their Bible, and specifically that He would come into Jerusalem on a donkey exactly 173,880 days (483 years) from the command to rebuild Jerusalem (Daniel 9:24, Ezra 1:2, Zechariah 9:9).

That was one incredibly specific prophecy! Jesus fulfilled it to the exact day. And the Jews missed it. It was there to read, and they missed it.

1st Coming Prophecies

Jesus continued to fulfill numerous other very specific prophecies like those on the next page:

OT Prophecy/NT Fulfillment

- *He was hated for no reason - Ps. 35:19 / Jn. 15:24*
- *He was betrayed by a friend - Ps. 41:9 / Lk. 22:47*
- *Betrayed for 30 silver coins - Zech. 11:12 / Mt. 26:15*
- *Crucified among criminals - Is. 53:12 / Mk. 15:27*
- *Pierced in hands and feet - Zech. 12:10 / Jn. 20:27*
- *His clothing gambled away - Ps. 22:18 / Mt. 27:35*
- *No broken bones - Ps. 34:20 / Jn. 19:33*
- *Pierced through His side - Zech. 12:10 / Jn. 19:34*
- *Buried with the rich - Is.53:9 / Mt. 27:57-60*

In all there are some 300 prophecies regarding the first coming of the Messiah, and they were **all fulfilled**, exactly/literally, as written. Proof positive that the Bible can literally be trusted as God's inspired words—word for word.

There are also scores of prophecies regarding Israel's future in the latter days. Consider these seven prophecies:

1. Israel would return to their homeland after being **scattered for about 2000 years**. (Hos. 6:1-2)
2. They would remain a **pure race** despite being scattered all over the earth. (Ezek. 38:8)
3. They would take over their **land** in a day. (Isa. 66:8)
4. They would have a **mighty army**. (Ezek. 37:10)
5. They would have **nuclear weapons**. (Zech. 14:12; Ezek. 39:11-16)
6. That when regathered the new nation would be a **problem to the whole world**. (Zech. 12:3)

7. That the generation that saw the above prophecies come together would see the **Messiah's return.** (Mt. 24:34)

Well, that "generation" would be us. We saw those things come together in 1967 when the Jews took over the Temple Mount. Therefore, this generation today will see the Messiah return. Awesome!

Second Coming Prophecies

There are also prophecies about what it will be like just **before the end of the Church Age.** The Church Age is defined as the time between the arrival (Pentecost) and departure (Rapture) of God's Holy Spirit Who permanently indwells Believers.

Those latter-day prophecies include:
- World moving toward a **one-world government.** (Rev. 13:12)
- **Television**/Images of one person can be seen worldwide. (Rev. 13:15)
- **Knowledge** will be increased. (Dan. 12:4)
- Persia (**Iran**) and Gog (**Russia**) will be Israel's enemies possessing **nuclear weapons.** (Ezek. 38,39)

- The account of God's **creation** in Genesis will be scorned. (2Pet. 3:4-6)

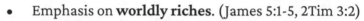

- Moving toward a **cashless society**. (Rev. 13:16-17)
- **Israel** will be a burdensome stone. (Zech. 12:3)
- Emphasis on **worldly riches**. (James 5:1-5, 2Tim 3:2)
- Ten countries of the **Old Roman Empire** will come together again. (Dan. 2:28, 41; Rev. 17:12)
- **Self** will be more important than God. (2Tim. 3:2-4)
- **World-wide** interconnected economy. (Rev. 18:11)

These are just a few of the prophecies concerning the days dead-ahead. Just as Jesus literally fulfilled the prophecies of His first coming, He will come again, literally fulfilling the recorded prophecies. You can bank on it!

CHAPTER SEVENTEEN

CLIMATE CHANGE IS REAL!

[We received a lot of static from people before they actually read the entire chapter!—Editor]

In 1958, noted liberal Betty Friedan wrote in *Harper's Magazine* that scientists were certain "the glacial thermostat, the present interglacial stage is well advanced; the earth is now heading into another Ice Age."

Since the late 1800s, establishment liberals proclaimed that our planet was doomed to freeze in as few as ten years. Referred to as "Global Cooling," the libs trotted out one scientist after another showing scientific research as proof of the coming "freeze." [1]

Yet since the early 1900s, scientists have disagreed as to whether the earth is heating up or cooling off.

(See the extensive climate change chronology that follows.)

- **1954** - "...winters are getting milder, summers drier. Glaciers are receding, deserts growing" - *US News and World Report*
- **1954** - "Climate - The Heat May Be Off" - *Fortune Magazine*
- **1959** - "Arctic Findings in Particular Support Theory of Rising Global Temperatures" - *New York Times*
- **1969** - "...the Arctic pack ice is thinning and the ocean at the North Pole may become an open sea within a decade or two" - *New York Times,* Feb. 20, 1969
- **1969** - "If I were a gambler, I would take even money that England will not exist in the year 2020" - **Paul Ehrlich** (while he now predicts doom from global warming, this quote only gets honorable mention, as he was talking about his crazy fear of overpopulation)
- **1970** - "...get a good grip on your long johns, cold weather haters - the worst may be yet to come...there's no relief in sight" - *Washington Post*
- **1974** - Global cooling for the past forty years - *Time Magazine*
- **1974** - "Climatological Cassandras are becoming increasingly apprehensive, for the weather aberrations they are studying may be the harbinger of another ice age" - *Washington Post*
- **1974** - "As for the present cooling trend a number of leading climatologists have concluded that it is very bad news indeed" - *Fortune* magazine, who won a Science Writing Award from the American Institute of Physics for its analysis of the danger.
- **1974** - "...the facts of the present climate change are such that the most optimistic experts would assign near certainty to major crop failure...mass deaths by starvation, and probably anarchy and violence" - *New York Times*
- **1975** - "Scientists Ponder Why World's Climate is Changing: A Major Cooling Widely Considered to Be Inevitable" - *New York Times,* May 21, 1975
- **1975** - "The threat of a new ice age must now stand alongside nuclear war as a likely source of wholesale death and misery for mankind: - Nigel Calder, editor, *New Scientist* magazine, in an article in *International Wildlife Magazine.*

- **1976 -** "Even U.S. farms may be hit by cooling trend" - *US News and World Report*
- **1981 -** Global Warming - "of an almost unprecedented magnitude" *New York Times*
- **1988 -** "I would like to draw three main conclusions. Number one, the earth is warmer in 1988 than at any time in the history of instrumental measurements. Number two, the global warming is now large enough that we can ascribe with a high degree of confidence a cause and effect relationship to the greenhouse effect. And number three, our computer climate simulations indicate that the greenhouse effect is already large enough to begin to effect the probability of extreme events such as summer heat waves - **Jim Hansen**, June 1988 testimony before Congress, see his later quotes and his superior's objection for context
- **1989 -** "On the one hand, as scientists we are ethically bound to the scientific method, in effect promising to tell the truth, the whole truth, and nothing but - which means that we must include all doubts, the caveats, the ifs, ands and buts. On the other hand, we are not just scientists but human beings as well. And like most people we'd like to see the world a better place, which in this context translates into our working to reduce the risk of potentially disastrous climate change. To do that we need to get some broad-based support, to capture the public's imagination. That, of course, means getting loads of media coverage. **So we have to offer up scary scenarios, make simplified, dramatic statements, and make little mention of any doubts we might have.** This "double ethical bind" we frequently find ourselves in cannot be solved by any formula. Each of us has to decide what the right balance is between being effective and being honest. I hope that means being both." **Stephen Schneider,** lead author of the Intergovernmental Panel on Climate Change, *Discover* magazine, October 1989.
- **1990 -** "We've got to ride the global warming issue. Even if the theory of global warming is wrong, we will be doing the right

thing - in terms of economic policy and environmental policy" -
Senator Timothy Wirth

- **1993 -** "Global climate change may alter temperature and rain-fall patterns, many scientists fear, with uncertain consequences for agriculture." *US News and World Report*

- **1998 -** No matter if the science [of global warming] is all pho-ny...climate change [provides] the greatest opportunity to bring about justice and equality in the world." **Christine Stewart,** Canadian Minister of the Environment, *Calgary Herald,* 1998

- **2001 -** Scientists no longer doubt that global warming is happening, and almost nobody questions the fact that humans are at least partly responsible - *Time* Magazine, Monday Apr. 9, 2001.

- **2009 -** *Climate change: melting ice will trigger wave of natural disasters.* Scientists at a London conference next week will warn of earthquakes, avalanches and volcanic eruptions as the atmosphere heats up and geology is altered. Even Britain could face being struck by tsunamis - "Not only are the oceans and atmosphere conspiring against us, bringing baking tempera-tures, more powerful storms and floods, but the crust beneath our feet seems likely to join in too," **Professor Bill McGuire,** director of the Benfield Hazard Research Centre, at University College London - *The Guardian,* Sept 2009

- **2010 -** "What Global Warming Looks Like." It was more than 5°C (about 10°F) warmer than climatology in the eastern Eu-ropean region including Moscow. There was an area in eastern Asia that was similarly unusually hot. The eastern part of the United States was unusually warm, although not to be degree of the hot spots in Eurasia. **James Hansen -** *NASA GISS,* Aug 11, 2010

- **2011 -** "Where Did Global Warming Go?" "In Washington, 'climate change' has become a lightning rod, it's a four-letter word," said **Andrew J. Hoffman,** director of the University of Michigan's Erb Institute for Sustainable Development - *New York Times,* Oct. 15, 2011

- **2012** - *Global warming close to becoming irreversible.* "This is the critical decade. If we don't get the curves turned around this decade we will cross those lines," said **Will Steffen,** executive director of the Australian National University's climate change institute, speaking at a conference in London. **Reuters,** Mar. 26, 2012
- **2013** - **"Global-warming 'proof' is evaporating."** The 2013 hurricane season just ended as one of the five quietest years since 1960. But don't expect anyone who pointed to last year's hurricanes as "proof" of the need to act against global warming to apologize; the warmists don't work that way. ***New York Post,*** Dec. 5, 2013
- **2014** - "Climate change: It's even worse than we thought." Five years ago, the last report of the intergovernmental Panel on Climate Change painted a gloomy picture of our planet's future. As climate scientists gather evidence for the next report, due in 2014, **Michael Le Page** gives seven reasons why things are looking even grimmer. *New Scientist* (undated in 2014)

By the 1980s, when the idiocy of the "fact" we're going to freeze showed obvious holes, they switched to "Global Warming" and have since paraded out more scientists with research showing the "irrefutable facts" of the coming world heat disaster.

But ultimately Global Warming began to also reveal its non-scientific stupidity, so they switched to "Climate Change."

THE POLITICAL CLIMATE

First it was:
"THE ICE AGE IS COMING"
Then is was:
GLOBAL WARMING
Now to cover all it's:
CLIMATE CHANGE!
But should be called:
PEOPLE CONTROL!

Now they're blaming all the world's problems on man's impact on the planet. They say there are "over 1000 research studies" that prove Climate Change is real... which is a bald-faced lie.

The national news promotes the lie, calling it the "FACT" of Climate Change, and comes down hard on anyone who disagrees. The only "FACT" is that these "studies" are myths, lies, and distortions produced by the same kind of people who conspired to say Donald Trump "colluded" with Russia.

> *...who can argue against saving our planet? All we have to do is give them the power...*

Yet students today are universally taught that it is a scientific fact that man (usually meaning white males) has so damaged this planet from using fossil fuels that the earth will last only a few more years... doom is coming soon if we don't do what they say.

To anyone with two brain cells, the obvious purpose of all these climate proclamations and predictions through the years is to use the climate for political value. After all, who can argue against saving our planet? All we have to do is give them the power to control more and more of our lives.

Liberal politicians are now turning up the heat saying we must change how we live, even saying if we don't change our ways we'll have to go back to the dark ages to stay alive on this planet.

Some politicians say this disaster will come in as few as 10 or 15 years. Of course, that's what they've been saying since the early 1900s: 10 to 15 years. It's a phrase well tested in those focus groups—makes people worry!

And this time they actually are right!

Yes, you read that correctly. The liberals are dead-on about climate change coming in the next 10 to 15 years. But it's not going to happen like they think.

One of the most graphic characteristics of the soon-coming Tribulation that follows the Rapture is the horrific scorching heat that comes on the earth, the temperature so high that people are grateful to die to escape the heat.

> *...these are the ones who come out of the great tribulation...they will hunger no longer, nor thirst anymore; nor will the sun beat down on them, nor any **heat**; Rev. 7:14, 16*

> *Men were scorched with fierce **heat**... Rev. 16:9*

This "climate change" will in fact sink Miami, as famously predicted by Bill Clinton when he said:

"'The water is going to keep rising' whether US stays in the Paris Accord Talks or not." (The Paris Accord was the world meeting, The Kyoto Accord/Protocols, to deal with Climate Change that President Trump wisely pulled out of soon after becoming President.)

And yes, the polar ice caps WILL melt—but probably in about an hour, not decades. And that will be the least of their problems. This is the time that God will shake the earth so violently that ALL the mountains will fall and ALL the islands will sink.

> ...and there was a great earthquake, such as there had not been since man came to be upon the earth, so great an earthquake was it, and so mighty. ... and every island fled away, and the mountains were not found. Rev. 16:18,20

In Isaiah 24:13,19 the Bible compares someone violently shaking an olive tree to get the olives to fall off to what God does to the earth during the Tribulation. Ouch!

All this causes the nations of the earth to be in disarray, totally baffled by all that is going on.

> There will be signs in sun and moon and stars, and on the earth dismay among nations, **in perplexity** at the roaring of the sea and the waves... Lk. 21:25

The bleeding-heart liberals left behind after the Rapture will have more than "climate change" to deal with...rather, they will be the recipients of God's wrath. God says the time will come when He will not be silent any more!

> I have kept silent for a long time, I have kept still and restrained Myself. Now like a woman in labor I will

groan, I will both gasp and pant. I will lay waste the mountains and hills and wither all their vegetation; I will make the rivers into coastlands and dry up the ponds. Isa. 42:14-15

Of course, God clearly warned of this time in His Word. It's there for anyone to read. He even offers a way to escape the coming horrors. But most people will choose to ignore Scripture and instead choose to worship Satan—who is actually behind all this hokey "climate change."And those who ignore the Word of God will pay a stiff price.

> *It's coming suddenly, in a moment they least expect it. The lies, murders, and blasphemy are all seen and recorded for future judgment.*

For the wrath of God is revealed from heaven against all ungodliness and unrighteousness of men who suppress the truth in unrighteousness... Rom 1:18

For it is because of these things that the wrath of God will come upon the sons of disobedience... Col. 3:6

Let me rephrase that in case you missed it. The WRATH of God IS coming against all unsaved sinners, all <u>non</u>-Believers. It's coming suddenly, in a moment they least expect it. The lies, murders, and blasphemy are all seen and recorded for future judgment.

It will be a sad time on earth.

> *...All the merry-hearted sigh. The gaiety of tambourines ceases, the noise of revelers stops, the gaiety of the harp ceases.... All joy turns to gloom. The gaiety of the earth is banished. Isa. 24:7, 8, 11*

Most will die. In the first half of the Seven-Year Tribulation, 50% of the earth's population dies. (Revelation 6:8, 9:18) In the second half of the Tribulation, most of the rest of the people die. Few will survive to live into the Millennium.

All born-again Believers will be removed from this earth before His judgment begins.

...Therefore, the inhabitants of the earth are burned, and few men are left. Isa. 24:6b

Praise the Lord that God has not appointed us to receive the coming "wrath!"

> *For God has **not destined us for wrath,** but for obtaining salvation through our Lord Jesus Christ... 1Thes 5:9*

> *Much more then, having now been justified by His blood, we shall be **saved from the wrath** of God through Him. Rom. 5:9*

All born-again Believers will be removed from this earth before His judgment begins.

So the next time some liberal starts in on "Climate Change," just say, "I agree with you, 'Climate Change' is coming." And that will give you one remarkable witnessing opportunity!

But keep in mind that this whole climate issue is not about the "climate." Rather, it's about "Control." In the not-too-distant future, this earth will be controlled by one person from one place. We're just seeing the beginnings of this taking shape.

Reference

1) https://en.wikipedia.org/wiki/Global_cooling

CHAPTER EIGHTEEN

ARE YOU BEING WATCHED... YET?

Imagine a world where everything you do is individually monitored, scored, and kept in a big database. And your personal score determines your lifestyle—what you can purchase, your ability to travel, the interest rate you pay at the bank, even your ability to rent an apartment or buy a home or be approved for a car loan.

Everything you do, or don't do, is monitored and scored. Your score also affects your family by causing your Internet to run more slowly and keeping you (and/or your kids) from the best schools and the best jobs. A low score could even land you in jail!

So in this imaginary world you have to be careful to keep your social score above a certain level or you could pay big consequences. You can't even get a driver's license without a decent social score. So if you're smart, you learn quickly what to do and what not to do.

Breaking the law in any way lowers your score. So will buying too much liquor in a month or using your Visa to purchase too many video games.

You also get lower scores for things like being late on a credit card payment or accessing a website that is in opposition to the ruling government party. Not to mention little things like jaywalking, or smoking on trains.

Posting opinions on social media that are not politically correct or posting lewd remarks or pictures will, of course, lower your score. Even bad habits like eating too much, parking in a no-parking area, and driving over the speed limit (yes, that too) are tracked daily and tallied.

EVERYTHING is watched and monitored. Your life is scored on a day-by-day basis. And in this world, a low score can even get you arrested and jailed for nothing more than having a low social score. All to keep you in compliance with the government's ideological framework.

Think this imaginary world I just described is absurd? Nope. Actually, this is what they are doing TODAY in China. Citizens there are 100% watched in order to be 100% controlled. The live camera system now monitors over a billion people and soon will cover/oversee all of China.

The Chinese government's system evaluates and scores you between 300 and 850 points. In addition to education, legal, banking, and employment, the score also takes into account perceived trustworthiness, security, wealth, consumption, and social networking (i.e., your online behavior, having "undesirable" friends, and even what you click on to "LIKE").

Due to low social scores, Chinese citizens are being "detained" (what we would call "arrested"). One man was chained to a chair for eight hours of interrogation for simply posting on Twitter... and Twitter is blocked in China!

> *Everything is watched and monitored. Your life is scored on a day-by-day basis...*

To use Twitter in China, you have to have special software to circumvent the Chinese government ban. But even then, the Chinese government watches posts worldwide, and there are many reports of thousands of private Chinese Twitter accounts disappearing with no explanation.

When I say they're watching everything, I mean everything. People have had their dogs taken away for their not being on a leash! When you get on a train, announcements are made to not misbehave or it will affect your social score. Of course you NEVER complain about the government.

China's data-driven technology is growing in leaps and bounds. Referred to as Cyberspace Governance, China not only blocks certain data on the Internet but it also tracks what you do click on to determine what they will let you

Chinese schools enforce 'smart uniforms' with GPS tracking to surveil students

do, and not do. You may not even know you are clicking on a site that will lower your score.

The Chinese government was tracking tourists crossing into China even before the COVID-19 "pandemic." The Border Police were beginning to seize smart phones from the X-ray security machines and installing an app called BXAQ. This app collects all personal information including text messages, event calendars, phone contacts, and lists of people called as well as what apps you're using.

They then check your data against a red-flag list of over 70,000 items. You're denied entry if you have, for instance, obvious things like bomb-making instructions. But the forbidden list also includes books written in Arabic, books (or materials or documents) about (or by) certain Christian groups deemed controversial, and documents relating to the Dalai Lama. Quite subjective, don't you think?

Cameras are everywhere as they've implemented the most sophisticated facial recognition system in the world. You can withdraw cash, check in at airports, and pay for goods using just your face. They not only read and verify individual faces, but also estimate age, ethnicity, and gender. But more importantly, they know where you are at all times.

There are 170 million cameras already in place, and 400 million more will be installed over the next three years. The system is so vast and accurate it's locating wanted suspects in real time.

At any moment in time, this system can match every face on the street with an ID card as well as the path of your car. It can trace these movements back seven days, matching you up with your relatives and the people you've seen this week.

They've even begun using facial recognition to determine moods of people — are they angry or happy? What is their sexuality? Are they walking too fast? In short, they can arrest people they THINK will commit a crime.

Nothing to Hide?

Chinese officials say if you have nothing to hide, you have nothing to fear. But as the technology develops, so does the potential for abuse. All humans are sinful. Can you imagine a Democrat-controlled American government in charge of deciding who gets dinged for what?

Using the social rating system, the Chinese have already banned 15 million people from traveling, buying property, or sending their kids to private school. And there's no reason to appeal if you get banned. You can appeal, but that just makes matters worse.

Since 2015, to put some teeth into the penalties, China has increased the number of police sixfold. Thousands of them have been equipped with face-scanning devices that can determine if you're a fugitive IN REAL TIME. This iron-fist approach is what they're using to control every single person in China.

> *"China is Doing the Right Things"*
>
> **Dr. Michael Ryan**
> EXECUTIVE DIRECTOR
> World Health
> Organization (WHO)
>
> NEWSWEEK 1/29/20

China has virtually become a total surveillance state where residents have different levels of freedom based on ethnicity, religious practices, and social score. The database for individuals includes things like your job, if you have a passport, even if you pray.

When all the scores are tallied, you're categorized into SAFE, REGULAR, or UNSAFE people. UNSAFE people are sent to study centers for political education. But these study centers are actually no more than prisons with walls, razor-wire barriers, and guard towers... you can't get out until they think you have changed your mind, realigned your politics, etc.

So people are basically being imprisoned based on surveillance data. And you can't even see your score or the data used to rate you. People are detained (arrested) and they have no idea where they're going or how long they will be there.

China Expands Its Surveillance Around The World

Two out of every three **drones** used around the world are manufactured by government-controlled Chinese companies. And consensus is that some 75% of U.S. government **security cameras** are manufactured in China.

Australia is currently wrestling with the overwhelming number of Chinese cameras in their cities and even military bases. Australian officials have determined that Chinese cameras are in use in their Army Forces Command, Air Force Air Command, Navy Strategic Command, and Army Special Operations HQ.

They're worried that China may actually be gaining access to the images and using the data to spy or even affect election results. The elephant-in-the-room concern is that Communist China can track Australia's entire military operation!

The Department of Homeland Security in the United States has been screaming about all this for years. Finally, in a rare bipartisan moment in the politics of Washington DC, Congress passed the National Defense Authorization Act, 2019, which prohibited cameras made by certain Chinese companies from being used in surveillance on U.S. soil. The reasoning was in part that China would be able to do surveillance in the U.S. as they suspect they've been doing in Australia.

The commonality of all this is that these cameras all use the Internet. Once online, the information is ripe for rip-off. And the cameras are made in a way that reprogramming can be done via the Internet. So what you determine to be safe today could be unsafe tomorrow.

This is just a foreshadowing of what's ultimately coming to the United States. Conservatives/Christians are already being unfairly targeted. Problems with the IRS targeting conservative/Christian groups were uncovered, and no one was held accountable. Imagine adding a social credit system like this used to shut up conservatives.

Again, this is happening today in China. How far away is this from the United States? Just recently Florida Democrat Congresswoman Frederica Wilson called for shutting down people who voice their opinion online saying, "We're gonna shut them down." Governmental surveillance used to control the population WILL come here too. And bummer for you if those who have control are not those whom you support.

> *Already there are social ratings beginning to be used in the US.*

It's Just a Matter of Time

Already there are social ratings beginning to be used in the United States. **The Palms Hotel** in Las Vegas is using a social media scoring system to provide perks to guests.

Twitter announced it is instituting a new social score for every user based on "influence." And Virgin Airlines has announced it will use these scores to determine upgrades and even pricing. And **Hoot Suite** announced it will allow you to sort your Twitter list based on the influence of your Twitter social score.

Tommy Hilfiger has begun embedding smart chips in some of its lines that are connected to an app where you (and the company) can track what you wear and where you wear it.

There have been four or five instances where a Compass post or advertisement was not approved because it didn't meet Facebook's policies. There was nothing untruthful with our ads, they just didn't like what we were posting! You can't tell people the truth... like the fact they are going to either heaven or hell! That's too cruel.

So most Believers easily see where this is going.

All This Is Clearly Prophesied in the Bible

The Bible says there will come a day when everyone on the earth who wants to eat or buy products will have to be part of a worldwide system. And this all-encompassing system will be run by none other than Satan himself.

> *And it was given to him to give breath to the image of the beast, so that the image of the beast would even speak and cause as many as do not worship the image of the beast to be killed. And he causes all, the small and the great, and the rich and the poor, and the free men and the slaves, to be given a mark on their right hand*

*or on their forehead, and he provides that **no one will be able to buy or to sell, except the one who has the mark**, either the name of the beast or the number of his name. Rev. 13:15–17*

John, through the inspiration of God's Holy Spirit, did an admirable job describing a clear reference to today. He'd been given a glimpse into the future of people watching their TVs, smart phones, and/or tablets and had to put it in his own vernacular. The screens could easily be what he described above as the "image of the beast."

After the Rapture, one day everyone will be controlled from one place. And the one who has control makes the rules. And the rule is simple… you either take the "Mark of the Beast" and get your food, or you don't take it and likely starve.

The Chinese have a system in place today that, between facial recognition, social monitoring, and an iron-clad grip on banking transactions, can in fact be expanded to control every person in the world. And if the Chinese can do this with 1.4 billion people, it's not a stretch to see this eventually being implemented in the U.S., Europe, etc.

So, knowing where all this is heading, we're definitely seeing the early stages of the worldwide system coming together. In 30AD people <u>voluntarily</u> worshiped Jesus when He was physically on earth for 3 1/2 years. There's coming a post-Rapture day when Satan dons the fake-Jesus attire and <u>forces</u> people to worship him for 3 1/2 years.

Some will take the Mark of the Beast, eat temporarily, and later go to hell.

> *...If anyone worships the beast and his image, and receives a mark on his forehead or on his hand, he also will drink of the wine of the wrath of God, ... and he will be tormented ...* **forever***. Rev. 14:9–11*

Forever is a long time, and many will choose poorly. But some will shine:

> *... behold, a great multitude which no one could count, from every nation and all tribes and peoples and tongues, standing before the throne and before the Lamb,* **clothed in white robes,** *and palm branches were in their hands; Rev. 7:9*

> **"...These are the ones who come out of the great tribulation,** *and they have washed their robes and*

made them white in the blood of the Lamb....They will hunger no longer, nor thirst anymore; nor will the sun beat down on them, nor any heat; for the Lamb ... will guide them to ...life; and God will wipe every tear from their eyes." Rev. 7:14–17

"...I saw the souls of those who had been beheaded because of their testimony of Jesus and because of the word of God, and those who had not worshiped the beast or his image, and had not received the mark on their forehead and on their hand; and they came to life and reigned with Christ for a thousand years." Rev. 20:4

Clearly, there will be those who miss the Rapture and immediately know what just happened. They will have the opportunity to be part of the greatest revival the earth has ever witnessed.[1]

Faced with the prospect of choosing temporary life with food or eternal life with no food, they choose wisely. Most will have to give up their earthly lives in order to have eternal life with Jesus. But certainly worth it.

"He is no fool who gives up what he can't keep in order to gain that which he cannot lose." Jim Elliot

References

1) https://compass.org/article-tribulation-evangelism-on-steroids-2/
- https://www.businessinsider.com/china-social-credit-system-punishments-and-rewards-explained-2018-4#6-getting-your-dog-taken-away-6

- https://www.nytimes.com/2019/01/10/business/china-twitter-censorship-online.html
- https://www.washingtonpost.com/politics/2019/03/21/what-do-people-china-think-about-social-credit-monitoring/?noredirect=on&utm_term=.648706d9ff1c
- https://www.businessinsider.com/china-social-credit-system-punishments-and-rewards-explained-2018-4
- https://www.pcmag.com/news/369368/china-is-installing-spyware-on-tourists-phones
- https://www.foxbusiness.com/retail/hilfiger-embeds-smart-chips-in-new-fashion-line

CHAPTER NINETEEN

SIGNS FOR THE SHEPHERDS
More to the Christmas Story

*And she gave birth to her firstborn son; and she wrapped Him in **cloths**, and laid Him in a **manger**, because there was no room for them in the inn. Lk. 2:7*

The birth of Jesus is an event most Christians know well. Joseph and Mary, who was nine months pregnant, had traveled from Nazareth to Bethlehem to register for a national census.

When they arrived in Bethlehem, they found there was no place for them to stay. Mary goes into labor, has her baby, and places Him in a manger.

One of the things you learn when you go to Israel is that our American conception of a "manger" is not very accurate. It certainly wasn't cute and wooden.

A "manger" was a "feeding trough," and they were always carved out of stone. They didn't make them out of wood because using them for food and water would cause them to rot. We see these feeding troughs all over Israel (see picture of my friend Cindy sitting in a stone manger).

*This will be a **sign** for you: you will find a baby wrapped in **cloths** and lying in a manger. Lk. 2:12*

We've written before about Jesus being born in Bethlehem in the middle of all those tens of thousands of sheep being born and raised for the Jewish Temple sacrifices.[1]

Jesus was even referred to by John the Baptist as the "Lamb of God." That would have been quite a statement to the Jews whose lives revolved around sacrificing lambs each year to cover their sins.

What Sign?

But to the shepherds in the fields, why did the angel of the Lord say the baby "wrapped in cloths" would be a sign? As it turns out, it was a HUGE sign!

In the time of Christ, during the birthing season, Levitical Priests would be sent from Jerusalem to Bethlehem to watch over the birthing process to make sure the sheep were born without any defects and not injured in the birthing process. Otherwise the animal might not be approved to be used as a sacrifice.

> *You shall not sacrifice to the LORD your God an ox or a sheep which has a blemish or any defect, for that is a detestable thing to the LORD your God. Deut. 17:1*

Since each Passover required tens of thousands of animals to sacrifice, it was important to birth as many as possible without injury.

On the edge of the fields surrounding Bethlehem where most of those sheep were being born, there was a two-story stone tower called the **Migdal Eder** tower. Israeli archaeologists recently found this tower. The picture is of the recent archaeological excavation.[2]

This tower is mentioned in the Book of Micah regarding the announcement of the birth of the Messiah.

*As for you, **tower of the flock**, Hill of the daughter of
Zion, To you it will come—Even the former dominion
will come, The kingdom of the daughter of Jerusalem."
Micah 4:8*

In plain English this is saying that the Messiah will be
revealed from the **Migdal Eder**—"the tower of the flock."

During the birthing season, the priests would climb the
tower and look out over all the flocks to see any signs a
sheep was about to give birth. Sheep usually get fidgety,
paw the ground and/or separate themselves from the flock
just before birthing a lamb.

> *If the lamb was
> born and found
> without blemish,
> it was immedi-
> ately wrapped in
> strips of cloth...*

When these signs were noticed,
they would bring the sheep to
the tower's ground floor where it
would give birth in a ceremonially
clean area.

If the lamb was born and found
without blemish, it was imme-
diately wrapped in strips of cloth made from old priestly
underwear.

The purpose was to make sure the lamb would stay un-
blemished. The priest would then put the lamb in a manger to keep it safe from getting trampled.

So when the angel of the Lord told the shepherds in the
field that the Savior had been born and the "sign" was that

He would be wrapped in the same cloths as the sacrificial sheep and placed in a manger, they would have immediately understood the significance of the "sign."

When the angels had gone away from them into heaven, the shepherds began saying to one another, "Let us go straight to Bethlehem then, and see this thing that has happened which the Lord has made known to us." So they came in a hurry and found their way to Mary and Joseph, and the baby as He lay in the manger. (Luke 2:15-16)

It's obvious that the shepherds knew exactly where to go with only limited info—they headed straight to the birthing tower where they found Joseph and Mary with Jesus lying where the newly born sacrificial sheep would lie.

> *The first clothes Jesus wore were the clothes of a priest!*

And, of course, don't miss the fact that the first clothes Jesus wore were the clothes of a priest!

So when you hear the Christmas story this year, we hope you have the chance to share, as Paul Harvey would say, "The rest of the story."

References
1) https://compass.org/article-all-that-blood
2) http://hethathasanear.com/Birth.html

CHAPTER TWENTY

RAPTURE IN THE 2030s?

I'm not a conspiracy theorist! At least, I don't worry about a man-based group that will someday take over the world and begin shooting Christians. I do know that a Satan-based world takeover WILL happen one day, but it's a post-Rapture event.

But I DO believe we're living in the last of the last days. And the Bible tells us to watch the signs — fulfilled prophecies... and there are many! The news these days sounds like a Bible-prophecy recap.

Therefore, we're obviously getting closer and closer to the end. And since we know the antichrist will show up in the last days and singularly rule the earth, we should very well be seeing things coming together just before the Church departs this earth.

We're so close that Satan has undoubtedly put people in place who are sold-out for him, setting the stage for his world takeover. No longer behind the scenes, they've come out in the open with their lies and deceit. For example:

UN Global Socialism Plan

In 2015, the United Nations had a huge Global Elites meeting in Paris, where all 193 countries of the world met and unanimously approved a plan to "Transform Our World" in the next 15 years. Dubbed UN Agenda 2030, they proudly outlined how they will use climate and global warming issues to take over the entire globe.

Obama's administration enthusiastically signed this monstrosity, in which it is specifically called a "plan of action for people, planet and prosperity by the year 2030."

This, of course, fit nicely with Obama's original campaign theme in 2008: "We want to fundamentally change America." They needed to change America because a free country didn't fit with a one-world government.

So before B.H.O. left office, he started a ball rolling that would have ultimately changed the U.S.A. from LEADING the world to FOLLOWING the U.N. The U.S.A. would then be under the U.N.'s direction to purportedly "save the earth." And if implemented, it would have been a disaster for Christians as it is a godless manifesto.

Realistically, this world "agenda" is nothing more than Satan ramping up for full control of the planet... and we know that's what WILL happen post-Rapture. When the Elites do finally reach their goals during the Tribulation, it'll be deadly to admit you're a Bible Believer.

But In Steps Donald Trump

Seeing through their Globalist ruse, President Trump is shaking up their agenda. He's not going along with any of it. Rather, he's making decisions that benefit America and making everyone else get in line.

This is making the Globalists white-hot mad, and they're unleashing everything they can to undermine his Presidency. It is unrelenting, and I think it's only the prayers from Believers that are keeping him alive.

The Elite control most of the media so we see a daily dose of political lies peppering the airwaves. Undeterred, under the prayer cover of millions from his Believer-base, the President continues to put America first.

Trade War or Common Sense?

For instance, the most recent "China Trade War" is simply making China trade fairly and equitably with the United States. The past four U.S. Presidents have allowed this trade imbalance to grow to such unhealthy levels that our whole U.S. monetary system is in serious jeopardy.

China's been taking their $700 billion surplus from the huge trade imbalance and purchasing hard assets like gold and silver, even gold and silver mines. President Trump sees this can't continue and must stop. And he's drawn a line in the sand.

Not Federal/Not Reserve

Another of President Trump's shot-over-the-bow salvos is to the Federal Reserve, which is neither "Federal" nor a "Reserve." Rather, it's a corporation controlled by eight Global Elite families. And President Trump is boldly in their face. Especially after the recent public comment by their Chairman, who said, "Trump needs to be defeated."[1]

> ## Satan is the
> ## *"god of this world"*
> ### 2Corinthians 4:4

This group of Global Elites, under the guise and power of "The Federal Reserve," has controlled our country's finances, milking us for over 100 years ...without accountability. Since they got control, our dollar has lost 92% of its value. They've never been audited so they basically do what they want to do.

President Trump again is just doing what is best for America. He's seriously looking at changing our dollar to a gold-backed dollar that would be trackable (think Bitcoin backed by gold). That would circumvent and free us from the Global Elite and the Federal Reserve all in one sweep.[2]

Regardless of all the good things our President is doing, we know this reprieve won't last forever. Most Christians realize that we're living in Satan's world. He IS the "god of this world," and he will one day get un-Holy-Spirit-hindered control.

But, thankfully, we're also in a God-controlled universe. And just like Nineveh was given an extra grace of time before God lowered the boom, we too are on borrowed time. We're in what the Bible calls the time of God's patience.[3]

Ultimately the end will come with the Church's exhilarating exit, which paves the way for Satan and his Global Elite minions to take over, ruling the earth for a horrific Seven-Year Tribulation period where literally one half of the earth's population is murdered.[4]

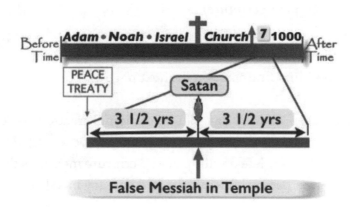

But the timing of the Devil's world takeover has been slowed down by God, for His unknown purposes. I personally think President Trump will be reelected to continue to keep America going on a non-global track. But at some point in the future, the Elites will get back in power and finish the job.

Now This Is What's Interesting

If President Trump is reelected, that would get us to 2024. We might get four more years, or even eight if a staunch conservative is elected following President Trump.

But even if Trump is not re-elected, this reprieve has pushed the Globalist agenda into the 2030s for completion. This is very interesting because that lines up very well with two end-time prophetic projections—the Church Age Prophecy and the One Generation Prophecy.

The 2000-Year Church Age Prophecy (see also Chapter 6: *Two Days in Scripture*)

We have taught and defended for years that God's original creation week is a timeline-template for all human time (see timeline chart on the next page).

The seven 24-hour days of God's original creation week are a template for 7000 years of time that God assigned to man to complete on this planet. Scripture mentions the correlation between 1000 years and one day in at least two places.

> *For a thousand years in Your sight are like yesterday when it passes by, or as a watch in the night.* Psa. 90:4

But do not let this one fact escape your notice, beloved, that with the Lord one day is like a thousand years, and a thousand years like one day. 2 Pet. 3:8

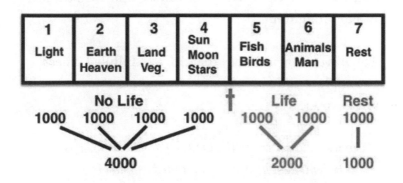

So applying this Creation week timeline of 1 day = 1000 years, the length of the Church Age is quite easy to see.

Looking at the above graphic, notice that no life was created on the first four 24-hour days of God's Creation week, only non-living things. And we know from the Bible's genealogy that there are about 4000 years between Adam and the cross.

At the end of the timeline, God's day of rest on the 7th day of the Creation week would correspond to Jesus' 1000-year millennial reign on earth when Satan is bound.

*And he laid hold of the dragon, the serpent of old, who is the devil and Satan, and bound him for **a thousand years**; Rev. 20:2*

*...reigned with Christ for **a thousand years**. Rev. 20:4*

That leaves two days, or 2000 years, for the Church Age in which we currently live. Jesus came to earth on the 5th day and brought life.

There is even a prophecy that can't be fulfilled unless this template-timeline for a 2000-year-old Church Age is true.

> *Come, let us return to the LORD. For He has torn us, but He will heal us; He has wounded us, but He will bandage us. He will revive us after **two days**; He will raise us up on the **third day**, that we may live before Him. Hos. 6:1–2*

That's an unfulfilled prophecy that says Israel will be scattered around the world for 2000 years (2 days), hurt and wounded. But after the 2000 years, God will revive them/bring them back to life. And on the third day, which is the last 1000 years, the Jews will literally live before Him in Israel.

It's also interesting that the only interaction anywhere in the Bible that Jesus had with non-Jews was specifically for **TWO DAYS.**

> *So when the Samaritans came to Jesus, they were asking Him to stay with them; and He stayed **there two days**. Jn. 4:40*

After the two days *He went forth from there into Galilee. Jn. 4:43*

After the "two days," on the "third day," He returned to the Jews. A perfect fit for the model. See also Exodus 19:10, 11—it will blow your mind.

So life showing up on the 5th and 6th days of the Creation week is a parallel to Jesus bringing life to the Church Age for 2000 years while the Jews are scattered, hurt and wounded.

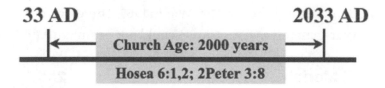

THEREFORE

The Church Age began in 33 AD with the coming of the Holy Spirit and will end with the Rapture, when the Holy Spirit departs. So, if our theory is correct, this would mean the Church Age would last until ROUGHLY 2033. This is not a prediction, just an observation!

There's also another prophetic application that points to the 2030s:

The "One Generation" Prophecy

Jesus said the generation who saw Israel come together in the latter days will not pass before seeing all the things listed in Matthew 24. A generation was referred to in varying lengths of times in the Bible—anywhere from 20 years to 100 years. Since seven and multiples of seven are God's numbers for completion, a 70-year generation isn't a stretch.

Mt. Moriah is the most important piece of property on earth as far as the Lord is concerned. It's where Abraham offered Isaac and the only place God allowed sacrifices to Him.

Israel didn't get back control of the Temple Mount/ Mt. Moriah until the Six-Day War in 1967. Therefore, the 70-year-generation countdown could not begin until 1967

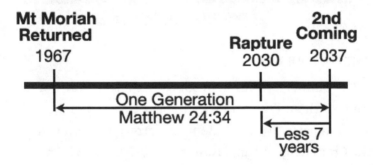

That puts us ROUGHLY at 2037. And if you subtract the seven-year tribulation, you get 2030. Again, not a prediction, only an observation based on Scripture.

Bottom Line

Therefore, between the Globalists trying to wrap things up in the 2030s, the Creation Week template pointing to

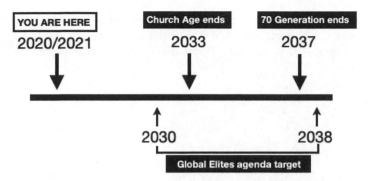

the 2030s, and the One Generation Prophecy pointing to the 2030s, you can make a good case that God has the Rapture scheduled for the 2030s. Certainly is interesting!

Of course (one more time) this is all speculation. We don't know for sure when the Lord will return. We can and do observe the signs. Hey, as we know, it could happen today!

For this reason you also must be ready; for the Son of Man is coming at an hour when you do not think He will. Matt. 24:44

So until that fateful day, use us, Lord! And watch over our President!

References:

1) https://www.japantimes.co.jp/news/2019/08/28/business/u-s-fed-help-defeat-trump-2020-not-enable-trade-war-china-ex-central-bank-official/#.XXlk5SV7lTY
2) https://qz.com/1646318/why-trump-and-judy-shelton-want-the-us-back-on-the-gold-standard/
https://investingnews.com/daily/resource-investing/precious-metals-investing/gold-investing/trump-gold-standard/

3) https://compass.org/article-gods-patience-in-the-last-days/
4) Rev. 6:8, 1/4 earth dies; Rev. 9:15, 1/3 of balance of earth's population dies. Total—1/2 population of earth dies during the Tribulation.

CHAPTER TWENTY ONE

MILLIONS MISSING?

If suddenly, in the blink of an eye, you find that a large number of people all over the earth have vanished into thin air, the following are important facts about what has just happened.

The Bible Predicted This Would Happen

Some 2,000 years ago, God prophesied in the Bible that a time would come when He would remove true Christians from the earth.

> *Behold, I tell you a mystery; we will not all sleep, but we will all be changed, **in a moment, in the twinkling of an eye**, at the last trumpet; for the trumpet will sound, and the dead will be raised imperishable, and we will be changed. For this perishable must put on the imperishable, and this mortal must put on immortality.*
> *1Cor. 15:51-53*

> *For the Lord Himself will descend from heaven with a shout, with the voice of the archangel and with the*

trumpet of God, and the dead in Christ will rise first.
*Then **we who are alive and remain will be caught***
up together with them in the clouds to meet the
***Lord in the air,** and so we shall always be with the*
Lord. 1Thess. 4:16-17

By predicting the future, it's proof the Bible is the only thing you can truly trust.

God's Purpose For This Mass Removal

God promised in the Bible that those who believed that His Messiah's shed blood paid for their sins wouldn't have to endure the seven years of terrible events that were also prophesied in the Bible and now coming on the people on earth.

...truly believe Jesus came from heaven to die as a sacrifice for your personal sins...

Therefore, only true Believers have been removed (sometimes called the Rapture). You are left behind because you didn't truly believe Jesus came from heaven to die as a sacrifice for your personal sins and was resurrected, defeating death.

Much more then, having now been justified by His blood, we shall be saved from the wrath of God through Him. Rom. 5:9

. . . Jesus, who rescues us from the wrath to come. 1Thess. 1:10

Thankfully God gave the world access to heaven through what the Jewish Messiah had provided VIA the cross. If you wish to also be rescued from the wrath that is coming on the earth, **believe** that Jesus is the Messiah who died to pay for your sins and rose from the grave, defeating death.

> *Truly, truly, I say to you, he who hears My word, and* ***believes*** *Him who sent Me, has eternal life, and does not come into judgment, but has passed out of death into life. Jn. 5:24*

> *Truly, truly, I say to you, he who believes has eternal life. Jn. 6:47*

> *Jesus said to her, "I am the resurrection and the life; he who believes in Me will live even if he dies..." Jn. 11:25*

If you confess with your mouth Jesus as Lord, and believe in your heart that God raised Him from the dead, you will be saved; for with the heart a person believes, resulting in righteousness, and with the mouth he confesses, resulting in salvation. (Romans 10:9-10)

> *And it shall be that* ***everyone who calls on the name of the Lord will be saved.*** *Acts 2:21*

> *These things I have written to you who believe in the name of the Son of God, so* ***that you may know that you have eternal life.*** *1Jn. 5:13*

So if you believe the good news that Jesus saved you from eternal damnation, find a Bible if you can and begin reading God's love story to mankind. Read Luke, Acts, and Ephesians to get started.

What Happens Next?

Even though you missed the "removal," if you now believe the good news of the gospel of Jesus by faith, you will escape the unquenchable and eternal fires of hell and immediately go to heaven when you die.

But the world is now under judgment and you very well may be killed for your faith. So the following is a guide for what's coming.

> *But the world is now under judgment and you very well may be killed for your faith.*

There are probably others who, like you, realize what has happened and now know the truth about God's Word. You should seek out these people as well as share this information with as many as you can. During these perilous times, you can really only trust the words in the Bible.

Below is a timeline of where we've been, where we are, and what's dead ahead—seven years of horrific tribulation.

*. . .behold, an ashen horse; . . .Death; and Hades. . . over
a **fourth of the earth, to kill** with sword and with
famine and with pestilence and by the wild beasts of the
earth. Rev. 6:8*

*. . .there will be a **great tribulation**, such as has not occurred since the beginning of the world until now, nor
ever will. Matt. 24:21*

After Jesus died on the cross, God's Holy Spirit came to
earth to indwell those who believed that Jesus' sinless
blood paid the price for their past, present, and future sins.

*But the Helper, the Holy Spirit, **whom the Father will
send** in My name, He will teach you all things...
Jn. 14:26*

*Now we have received, not the spirit of the world, but
the Spirit who is from God, so **that we may know the
things freely given to us by God...** 1Cor. 2:12*

The Holy Spirit also restrains wholesale evil on the earth.

*...the mystery of lawlessness is already at work; only He
[the Holy Spirit] who now restrains will do so until He
is taken out of the way. 2Thess. 2:7*

But God's Spirit was removed from the earth prior to the
Seven Years of Tribulation, a time of God's judgment on
earth. That's why millions just disappeared—all who had

the Spirit of God living in them, who were alive at the time of His departure, were simultaneously removed from the earth with Him (The Holy Spirit).

When the Holy Spirit left, they left with Him!

For He Himself has said, "I WILL NEVER DESERT YOU, NOR WILL I EVER FORSAKE YOU..." Heb. 13:5

God's Purpose For The Seven-Year Tribulation

The next Seven Years of Tribulation is also known as "the time of Jacob's distress" (Jeremiah 30:7) because Israel will come back into God's focus for the world to see. It will be obvious that Israel is God's chosen nation on earth.

My holy name I will make known in the midst of My people Israel; and I will not let My holy name be profaned anymore. And the nations will know that I am the LORD, the Holy One in Israel. Ezek. 39:7

The LORD has made known His salvation; He has revealed His righteousness in the sight of the nations. He has remembered His lovingkindness and His faithfulness to the house of Israel. . . Psa. 98:2-3

Some 2000 years ago **Israel rejected their Messiah** and therefore God blinded them during the Church Age period that followed Jesus' crucifixion.

...a partial hardening has happened to Israel until the
fullness of the Gentiles has come in; Rom. 11:25

The recent disappearance of the true Christians is proof
that God is now again making Israel His primary focus on
the earth.

God has not rejected His people whom He foreknew.
Rom. 11:2

People On Earth Now Have A Choice

After the removal of the Believers, people who are alive
and remain have a clear-
cut decision to make—you
can choose God or Satan.
People will either choose
to believe the false signs
and wonders by Satan—or
eternal salvation offered via
Jesus Christ.

> *After the removal of the*
> *Believers, people who*
> *are alive and remain*
> *have a clear-cut deci-*
> *sion to make...*

The one whose coming is in accord with the activity
of Satan, with all power and signs and false wonders,
and with all the deception of wickedness for those who
perish, because they did not receive the love of the truth
so as to be saved. 2 Thess. 2:9-10

Those who do not trust God's Word will fall for Satan's
lie and be doomed to **hell forever**.

*For this reason God will send upon them a deluding influence so that **they will believe what is false**, in order that they all may be judged who did not believe the truth, but took pleasure in wickedness. 2Thess. 2:11-12*
*So it will be at the end of the age; the angels will come forth and take out the wicked from among the righteous, and will throw them into the **furnace of fire**; in that place there will be weeping and gnashing of teeth. Matt. 13:49-50*

*These will pay the penalty of **eternal** destruction... 2Thess. 1:9*

The following is a list of major events predicted in the Bible that will happen in the near future, in their probable order:

• Many Nations Attack Israel

Soon, if it hasn't happened already, many nations will come against Israel to steal her riches.

*You will go up, you will come like a storm; you will be like a cloud covering the land, you and all your troops, and **many peoples** with you. Ezek. 38:9*

*Have you come to capture spoil? Have you assembled your company to seize plunder, to carry away **silver and gold**, to take away cattle and goods, **to capture great spoil?** Ezek. 38:13*

The countries attacking Israel are:
- Gog, prince of Rosh, Meshech and Tubal (Ezek. 38:3)
- Persia, Ethiopia and Put (Ezek. 38:5)
- Gomer, Beth-togarmah (Ezek. 38:6)

It's hard to predict with absolute certainty who these attacking nations will be, but Russia (Gog) and Iran (Persia) are likely to be two of them.

• Israel Is Victorious

Israel will have a huge victory over the invading nations and the world will see that God Himself is protecting Israel.

"It will come about on that day, when Gog comes against the land of Israel," declares the Lord GOD, *"that My fury will mount up in My anger." Ezek. 38:18*

Israel will have a huge victory over the invading nations.

*"**I will strike your bow from your left hand and dash down your arrows from your right hand.** You will fall on the mountains of Israel, you and all your troops and the peoples who are with you; I will give you as food to every kind of predatory bird and beast of the field. You will fall on the open field; for it is I who have spoken," declares the Lord GOD. Ezek. 39:3-5*

"...I will magnify Myself, sanctify Myself, and make Myself known in the sight of many nations; and they will know that I am the LORD." Ezek. 38:23

- **World War, Death, Famine and Cataclysmic Events**

With God's Holy Spirit having been removed, Who is called "the Restrainer" of unrelenting evil, the world is aflame.

*For then there will be a **great tribulation**, such as has not occurred since the beginning of the world until now, nor ever will. Matt. 24:21*

Seemingly out of nowhere, a man steps forward...

*...And there will be a **time of distress such as never occurred** since there was a nation until that time... Dan. 12:1*

*The first sounded, and there came hail and fire, mixed with blood, and they were thrown to the earth; and a third of the earth was burned up, and **a third of the trees were burned up**, and all the green grass was burned up. Rev. 8:7*

- **Emergence of a World Leader**

Seemingly out of nowhere, a man steps forward who sounds like he can save the world.

*I looked, and behold, a white horse, and he who sat on it had a bow; and a crown was given to him, and **he went out conquering** and to conquer. Rev. 6:2*

*. . . **the man of lawlessness** is revealed, the son of destruction, who opposes and exalts himself above every so-called god or object of worship... 2Thess. 2:3-4*

*He will speak out against the Most High and wear down the saints of the Highest One, and he will intend to **make alterations in times and in law**... Dan. 7:25*

• New World Leader Calls for Peace

This world leader orchestrates a seven-year peace treaty between 10 nations and Israel. This begins the seven years of prophesied tribulation.

And he will make a firm covenant with the many for one week [seven years], but in the middle of the week he will put a stop to sacrifice and grain offering...
Dan. 9:27

There was given to him a mouth speaking arrogant words and blasphemies, and authority to act for forty-two months was given to him. Rev. 13:5

*They have healed the brokenness of My people superficially, saying, **"Peace, peace," but there is no peace.**
Jer. 6:14*

• A New Worldwide Economic Order is Instituted

The New World Leader will gain more and more power as he institutes a global economic system. The Bible gives specific warnings about this system that have eternal ramifications.

*** Refuse the Mark! ***

Those alive today will soon be told that they can stay alive only by joining the world system and voluntarily receiving an identifying mark on their body.

And he [the leader of the new world] causes all, the small and the great, and the rich and the poor, and the free men and the slaves, to be given a mark on their right hand or on their forehead, and he provides that **no one will be able to buy or to sell, except the one who has the mark,** *either the name of the beast or the number of his name. Rev. 13:16-17*

...if you choose to join the world in order to live... you will receive horrific plagues...

God warns not to take this mark because if you choose to join the world system in order to live longer on earth, you will receive horrific plagues from angels in the sky.

So the first angel went and poured out his bowl on the earth; and it became a loathsome and malignant sore **on the people who had the mark** *of the beast and who worshiped his image. Rev. 16:2*

And worst of all, if you take that mark, when you die you'll be cast into a punishing hell for eternity.

. . . If anyone . . . receives a mark on his forehead or on his hand, he also will drink of the wine of the wrath of God, which is mixed in full strength in the cup of His anger; and he will be tormented with fire and brimstone in the presence of the holy angels and in the presence of the Lamb. And the smoke of their torment goes up forever and ever; they have no rest day and night, those who worship the beast and his image, and whoever receives the mark of his name. Rev. 14:9-11

[NOTE: If you're reading this before the humanity removal has taken place, and the Internet is still working, you can view a simple but complete overview of the entire Bible in 30 minutes at: compass.org/30]

Bottom Line: Don't Believe the Lies

Those who are now in power are going to lie to you about many things. Watch for these three big lies:

Lie #1:
About what happened to all those people who vanished.

> **Truth:**
> They're fine, God removed them, they're in heaven.

Lie #2
About why you need to take the "Mark of the Beast."

> **Truth:**
> Don't, because if you do, you'll go to hell FOREVER!

Lie #3
About the people of Israel being your enemy.

> **Truth:**
> They're not, they're God's chosen people whom He loves.

This is a difficult time to live

Standing against the earth-shaking evil powers will be difficult. And life as a Believer in Jesus during this time won't be easy. Quite frankly, you may very well be killed. But God promises that even though you may die on earth standing on your faith, you'll go straight to heaven for eternity.

> *Then one of the elders answered, saying to me, "These who are clothed in the white robes, who are they, and* **where have they come from?"** *I said to him, "My lord, you know." And he said to me,* **"These are the ones who come out of the great tribulation, and they have washed their robes and made them white in the blood of the Lamb.** *For this reason, they are before the throne of God; and they serve Him day and night in His temple; and He who sits on the throne will spread His tabernacle over them.* **They will hunger no longer, nor thirst anymore; nor will the sun beat down on them, nor any heat;** *for the Lamb in the center of the throne will be their shepherd, and will guide them to springs of the water of life; and* **God will wipe every tear from their eyes."** *Rev. 7:13-17*

*. . . I saw the souls of those who had been beheaded because of their testimony of Jesus and because of the word of God, and those **who had not worshiped the beast or his image, and had not received the mark on their forehead and on their hand; and they came to life and reigned with Christ for a thousand years.** Rev. 20:4*

So there's incredible hope for you and anyone else who believes the good news that Jesus offers salvation from eternal damnation. If you believe the good news that Jesus died for your sins, He will save you from the eternal fires of hell.

It is a trustworthy statement, deserving full acceptance, that Christ Jesus came into the world to save sinners... 1Tim. 1:15

> *...He will save you from the eternal fires of hell.*

Seven Scriptural Truths That Affect Your Eternity

1) It is a fact that God loves you.

*For God so loved the world, that He gave His only begotten Son, that whoever believes in Him shall not perish, but have **eternal** life. For God did not send the Son into the world to judge the world, but that the world might be saved through Him. Jn. 3:16-17*

2) It is a fact that you're a sinner.

*...for **all** have sinned and fall short of the glory of God. Rom. 3:23*

If we say that we have no sin, we are deceiving ourselves and the truth is not in us. 1 Jn. 1:8

3) It is a fact that sin separates you from God and heaven.

*...the wages of sin is **death**... Rom. 6:23*

4) It is a fact that Jesus paid the price to redeem you from sin.

...that the world might be saved through Him.

*God demonstrates His own love toward us, in that while we were yet sinners, Christ died for us. Much more then, having now been justified by His blood, we shall be **saved from the wrath** of God through Him. Rom 5:8-9*

*. . . the blood of Jesus His Son cleanses us from **all** sin. 1 Jn. 1:7*

5) It is a fact that you can be saved from eternity in hell.
If you believe the good news of what God has done for you–that God sent His Son from heaven to shed His blood in death to pay the price for your personal sins and

that He rose from the dead, defeating death–you will be saved by faith.

> *If you confess with your mouth Jesus as Lord, and **be-***
> ***lieve** in your heart that God raised Him from the dead,*
> *you will be saved;... Rom. 10:9*

> *...**Believe** in the Lord Jesus, and you will be saved.*
> *Acts 16:31*

6) It is a fact that if you're now a Believer, you're saved by what He did, not what you do or don't do.

> *For by grace you have been saved through faith; and*
> *that not of yourselves, it is the gift of God; **not as a re-***
> ***sult of works**, so that no one may boast. Eph. 2:8-9*

7) If you are now a Believer, Satan hates you. You're not up against bad people, but rather the evil that is behind them.

> *Finally, be strong in the Lord and in the strength of His*
> *might. Put on the full armor of God, so that you will*
> *be able to stand firm against the schemes of the devil.*
> ***For our struggle is not against flesh and blood, but***
> ***against the rulers, against the powers, against the***
> ***world forces of this darkness, against the spiritual***
> ***forces of wickedness in the heavenly places.** There-*
> *fore, take up the full armor of God, so that you will be*
> *able to resist in the evil day, and having done every-*
> *thing, to stand firm. Eph. 6:10-13*

Although you may be tremendously confused about the events currently surrounding you, try to find a Bible because it has God's truth that you can trust.

Be wise, refuse the mark and live for Him! Because eternity is a LONG, LONG time!